Disruptive Possibilities: How Big Data Changes Everything

Jeffrey Needham

O'REILLY®

Beijing · Cambridge · Farnham · Köln · Sebastopol · Tokyo

Table of Contents

CHAPTER 1

The Wall of Water

And Then There Was One

And then there was one—one ecosystem, one platform, one community—and most importantly, one force that retrains vendors to think about customers again. Welcome to the tsunami that Hadoop, noSQL, and all internet-scale computing represents. Some enterprises, whose businesses don't appear to be about data at all, are far from the shoreline where the sirens are faint. Other organizations that have been splashing around in the surf for decades now find themselves watching the tide recede rapidly. The speed of the approaching wave is unprecedented, even for an industry that has been committed, like any decent youth movement, to innovation, self-destruction, and reinvention. Welcome to the future of computing. Welcome to big data. Welcome to the end of computing as we have known it for 70 years.

Big data is a type of supercomputing for commercial enterprises and governments that will make it possible to monitor a pandemic as it happens, anticipate where the next bank robbery will occur, optimize fast food supply chains, predict voter behavior on election day, and forecast the volatility of political uprisings while they are happening. The course of economic history will change when, not if, criminals stand up their Hadoop clusters. So many seemingly diverse and unrelated global activities will become part of the big data ecosystem. Like any powerful technology, in the right hands, it propels us toward limitless possibilities. In the wrong hands, the consequences can be unimaginably destructive.

The motivation to get big data is immediate for many organizations. If a threatening organization gets the tech first, then the other organization is in serious trouble. If Target gets it before Kohl's or the Chinese navy gets it before the US navy or criminal organizations get it before banks, then they will have a powerful advantage. The solutions will require enterprises to be innovative at many levels, including technical, financial, and organizational. As in the 1950s during the cold war, whoever masters big data will win the arms race, and big data is the arms race of the 21st century.

Commercial Supercomputing Comes of Age

Trends in the computing industry mimic those of fashion—if you wait long enough, you will wear it again. Many of the technologies found in big data have been circulating in the industry for decades, such as clustering, parallel processing, and distributed file systems. Commercial supercomputing originated with companies operating at internet scale that needed to process ever-increasing numbers of users and their data (Yahoo! in the 1990s, then Google and Facebook). However, they needed to do this quickly and economically—in other words, affordably at scale. This is internet-scale commercial supercomputing, more commonly known as big data.

Big data will bring disruptive changes to organizations and vendors, and will reach far beyond networks of friends to the social network that encompasses the planet. But with those changes come possibilities. Big data is not just this season's trendy hemline; it is a must-have piece that will last for generations.

A Stitch in Time

Large-scale computing systems are not new. Weather forecasting has been a nasty big data problem since the beginning, when weather models ran on a single supercomputer that could fill a gymnasium and contained a couple of fast (for the 1970s) CPUs with very expensive memory. Software in the 1970s was primitive, so most of the performance at that time was in the clever hardware engineering.

By the 1990s, software had improved to the point where a large program running on monolithic supercomputers could be broken into a hundred smaller programs working at the same time on a hundred workstations. When all the programs finished running, their results were stitched together to form a week-long weather simulation. Even in the 1990s, the simulators used to take fifteen days to compute seven days of weather. It really didn't help farmers to find out that it rained last week. Today, the parallel simulations for a weeklong forecast complete in hours.

As clairvoyant as weather forecasting appears to be, those programs can't predict the future; they attempt to simulate and model its behavior. Actual humans do the forecasting, which is both art and supercomputing craft. Most weather forecasting agencies use a variety of simulators that have different strengths. Simulators that are good at predicting where a waterspout will make landfall in Louisiana are not so great at predicting how the morning marine layer will affect air operations at San Francisco International. Agency forecasters in each region pore over the output of several simulations with differing sets of initial conditions. They not only look at actual data from weather stations, but also look out the window (or the meteorological equivalent—Doppler radar).

Although there is a lot of data involved, weather simulation is not considered "Big Data" because it is so computationally intense. Computing problems in science (including meteorology and engineering) are also known as high-performance computing (HPC) or scientific supercomputing. The very first electronic computers were doing scientific computing, such as calculating trajectories of missiles or cracking codes, all of which were mathematical problems involving the solution of millions of equations. Scientific computing also solves equations for "non-scientific" problems such as rendering animated films.

Big data is the commercial equivalent of HPC, which could also be called high-performance commercial computing or commercial supercomputing. Big data can also solve large computing problems, but it is less about equations and more about discovering patterns. In the 1960s, banks first used commercial computers for automating accounts and managing their credit card business. Today companies such as Amazon, eBay, and large bricks-and-mortar retailers use commercial supercomputing to solve their internet-scale business problems, but commercial supercomputing can be used for much more than analyzing bounced checks, discovering fraud, and managing Facebook friends.

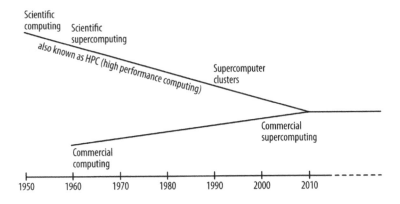

The Yellow Elephant in the Room

Hadoop is the first commercial supercomputing software platform that works at scale and is affordable at scale. Hadoop exploits the parlor trick of parallelism already well established in the HPC world. It was developed in-house at Yahoo! to solve a very specific problem, but they quickly realized its potential to tackle many other internet-scale computing problems. Although Yahoo!'s fortunes have changed, it made a huge and lasting contribution to the incubation of Google, Facebook, and Big Data.

Hadoop was originally created to affordably process Yahoo!'s flood of clickstream data, the history of the links a user clicks on. Since it could be monetized to prospective advertisers, analysis of clickstream data from tens of thousands of servers required an internet-scale database that was economical to build and operate. Yahoo! found most commercial solutions at the time were either incapable of scaling or unaffordable if they could scale, so Yahoo! had to build it from scratch, and DIY commercial supercomputing was born.

Like Linux, Hadoop is an open-source software technology. Just as Linux spawned commodity HPC clusters and clouds, Hadoop has created a big data ecosystem of new products, old vendors, new start-ups, and disruptive possibilities. Because Hadoop is portable, it is not just available on Linux. The ability to run an open source product like Hadoop on a Microsoft operating system is significant and a triumph for the open source community—a wild fantasy only 10 years ago.

Scaling Yahoovians

Because Yahoo! was the first internet-scale company, understanding their history is key to understanding big data's history. Jerry Yang and Dave Filo started Yahoo! as a project to index the web, but the problem grew to the point where conventional strategies simply could not keep up with the growth of content that needed to be indexed. Even before Hadoop came along, Yahoo! required a computing platform that always took the same amount of time to build the web index however large the web grew. Yahoo! realized they needed to borrow the parallelism trick from the HPC world to achieve scalability, and then Yahoo!'s computing grid became the cluster infrastructure that Hadoop was subsequently developed on.

Just as important as the technology that Yahoo! developed was how they reorganized their Engineering and Operations teams to support computing platforms of this magnitude. Yahoo!'s experience operating a massive computing plant that spread across multiple locations led them to reinvent the IT department. Complex platforms need to be initially developed and deployed by small teams. Getting an organization to scale up to support these platforms is an entirely different matter, but that reinvention is just as crucial as getting the hardware and software to scale.

Like most corporate departments from HR to Sales, IT organizations traditionally achieved scalability by centralizing skills. There is no question that having a small team of experts managing a thousand storage arrays is more cost effective than paying the salaries for a huge team, but Storage Admins don't have a working knowledge of the hundreds of applications on those arrays. Centralization trades generalist working knowledge for cost efficiency and subject matter expertise. Enterprises are finally starting to understand the unintended consequences of trade-offs made long ago that produced silos that will inhibit their ability to implement big data.

Traditional IT organizations partition expertise and responsibilities, which constrains collaboration between and among groups. Small errors due to misunderstandings might be tolerable on few small email servers, but small errors on production supercomputers can cost corporations a lot of time and money. Even a 1% error can make a huge difference. In the world of big data, 300 terabytes is merely Tiny Data, but a 1% error in 300 terabytes is 3 million megabytes. Finding and fixing errors at this scale can take countless hours. Yahoo! learned what the HPC community that has been living with large clusters for about 20 years knows. They learned that a small team with a working knowledge of the entire platform works best. Silos of data and responsibility become impediments in both scientific supercomputing and commercial supercomputing.

Internet-scale computing plants work because early practitioners learned a key lesson: supercomputers are finely tuned platforms that have many interdependent parts and don't operate as silos of processing. Starting in the 1980s, however, customers were encouraged to view the computing platform as a stack with autonomous layers of functionality. This paradigm was easier to understand, but with increasingly complex platforms, the layer metaphor began to cognitively mask the underlying complexity that hindered or even prevented successful triage of performance and reliability problems. Like an F1 racing platform or a Boeing 737, supercomputer platforms must be understood as a single collection of technologies or the efficiency and manageability will be impaired.

Supercomputers Are Platforms

In the early history of the computer industry, systems were platforms —they were called mainframes and typically came from a company that also supplied a dedicated group of engineers in white shirts and ties who worked alongside their customers to ensure the platform performed when they handed over the keys. This method was successful as long as you enjoyed being an IBM customer—there has always been a fine line between "throat to choke" and monopoly arrogance. After IBM crossed this line in the 1960s, the resulting industry offered more choice and better pricing, but it became an industry of silos.

Today, companies that dominate their silo still tend to behave like a monopoly for as long as they can get away with it. As database, server, and storage companies proliferated, IT organizations mirrored this alignment with corresponding teams of database, server, and storage experts. However, in order to stand up a big data cluster successfully, every person who touches or works on the cluster must be physically and organizationally close to one another. The collaborative teamwork required for successful cluster deployments at this scale never, ever happens in a sub-silo of a silo.

If your company wants to embrace big data or gather in that magical place where Big Data Meets The Cloud, the IT organization will have to tear down some silos and become more aware of the platform. Unfortunately, most organizations do not handle any change well, let alone rapid change. Chaos and disruption have been constants in this industry, yet were always accompanied by possibility and innovation. For enterprises that are willing to acknowledge and prepare for the wall of water, big data will be a cleansing flood of new ideas and opportunities.

Big Data! Big Bang!

As the big data ecosystem evolves over the next few years, it will inundate vendors and customers in a number of ways.

First, the disruption to the silo mentality, both in IT organizations and the industry that serves them, will be the Big Story of big data.

Second, the IT industry will be battered by the new technology of big data because many of the products that predate Hadoop are laughably unaffordable at scale. Big data hardware and software is *hundreds* of times faster than existing enterprise-scale products and often *thousands* of times cheaper.

Third, technology as new and disruptive as big data is often resisted by IT organizations because their corporate mandate requires them to obsess about minimizing OPEX and not tolerate innovation, forcing IT to be the big bad wolf of big data.

Fourth, IT organizations will be affected by the generation that replaces those who invested their careers in Oracle, Microsoft, and EMC. The old adage "no one ever gets fired for buying (historically) IBM" only applies to mature, established technology, not to immature, disruptive technology. Big data is the most disruptive force this industry has seen since the introduction of the relational database.

Fifth, big data requires data scientists and programmers to develop a better understanding of how the data flows underneath them, including an introduction (or reintroduction) to the computing platform that makes it possible. This may be outside of their comfort zones if they are similarly entrenched within silos. Professionals willing to learn new ways of collaborating, working, and thinking will prosper, and that prosperity is as much about highly efficient and small teams of people as it is about highly efficient and large groups of servers.

Sixth and finally, civil liberties and privacy will be compromised as technology improvements make it affordable for any organization (private, public, or clandestine) to analyze the patterns of data and behavior of anyone who uses a mobile phone.

Endless Possibilities

Today, big data isn't just for social networking and machine-generated web logs. Agencies and enterprises will find answers to questions that they could never afford to ask and big data will help identify questions that they never knew to ask.

For the first time, car manufacturers can afford to view their global parts inventory spread over hundreds of plants and also collect the petabytes of data coming from all the sensors that are now in most vehicles. Other companies will be able to process and analyze vast amounts of data while they are still in the field collecting it. Prospecting for oil involves seismic trucks in the field collecting terabytes of data. Previously, the data was taken back to an expensive datacenter and transferred to expensive supercomputers, which took a lot of expensive time to process. Now a Hadoop cluster spread over a fleet of trucks sitting in a motel parking lot could run a job overnight that provides guidance on where the next day's prospecting should take place. In the next field over, farmers could plant thousands of environmental sensors that transmit data back to a Hadoop cluster running in a barn to "watch" the crops grow. Hadoop clusters make it more affordable for government agencies to analyze their data. The WHO and CDC will be able to track regional or global outbreaks like H1N1 and SARS almost as they happen.

Although big data makes it possible to process huge data sets, it is parallelism that makes it happen quickly. Hadoop can also be used for data sets that don't qualify as big data, but still need to be processed in parallel. Think about a tiny Hadoop cluster running as an artificial retina.

Whether the wall of data arrives in the form of a tsunami, monsoon, or even a fog, it must be collected into a commonly accessible and affordable reservoir so that many of these possibilities can be realized. This reservoir cannot be yet another drag-and-drop enterprise data warehouse pyramid schema. The data contained in this reservoir, like the fresh water found in real reservoirs, must sustain the future life of the business.

Disruptive and opportunistic, big data is thrusting computer science away from the classic John von Neumann style of computing—where we finally stop looking at every piece of hay in the millions of haystacks that big data makes possible and move toward a new form of spatial supercomputing. Long before those steps are taken, big data will change the course of history.

CHAPTER 2

Big Data: The Ultimate Computing Platform

Introduction to Platforms

A platform is a collection of sub-systems or components that must operate like one thing. A Formula One racing vehicle (which drivers refer to as their platform) is the automobile equivalent of a supercomputer. It has every aspect of its design fully optimized not simply for performance, but performance per liter of gas or kilogram of curb weight. A 2-litre engine that creates 320HP instead of 140HP does so because it is more efficient. The engine with higher horsepower does have better absolute performance, but performance really means efficiency—like HP/KG and miles/gallon, or with computing platforms, jobs executed/watt. Performance is always measured as a ratio of something being accomplished for the effort expended.

The descendant of Honda's F1 technology is now found in other cars because optimized technology derived from the racing program enabled Honda to design more powerful vehicles for consumers. A Honda Civic is just as much a platform as the F1. The engine, brakes, steering, and suspension are designed so it feels like you're driving a car, not a collection of complex sub-components. Platforms can span rivers, serve ads for shoes, and reserve seats on another notable platform—the kind with wings.

Come Fly with Me

The design and development of a new commercial aircraft is complex, costly, and tangled in regulations, making the process justifiably slow since design flaws can leave bodies scattered across the infield. Platforms that must be manufactured out of physical components require more planning than platforms that are manufactured out of nothing —such as software—because a new set of engines can't be downloaded every week. However, modern aircraft designers understand the value of that flexible software stuff. First introduced in military fighters, "fly-by-wire" technology refers to flying by electrical wire, not mechanical wire (like bicycle brake cables). In traditional aircraft, the stick and pedals were mechanically connected to the control surfaces on the wings, so mechanical linkages controlled those surfaces. In a fly-by-wire aircraft, the controls in the cockpit are inputs to a computer, which controls motorized actuators that move the surfaces on the wings and tail.

Fly-by-wire software is also used to prevent fighter pilots from flying into unconsciousness. Pilots can bank into turns so steep that they could black out, but software detects those conditions and limits turns to keep pilots conscious and alive. Similar features apply to commercial aircraft and sport sedans, making those platforms safer and more efficient. Unfortunately, if the fly-by-wire software (which is very easy to change and "improve") has bugs or design flaws, this can still result in that mess on the infield that they prefer to avoid.

Computing Platforms

In the 1960s, Bank of America and IBM built one of the first credit card processing systems. Although those early mainframes processed just a fraction of the data compared to that of eBay or Amazon, the engineering was complex for the day. Once credit cards became popular, processing systems had to be built to handle the load and, more importantly, handle the growth without constant re-engineering. These early platforms were built around mainframes, peripheral equipment (networks and storage), and software, all from a single vendor. IBM also built a massive database system as a one-off project for NASA during the Apollo program, which later evolved into a product called IMS. Because IBM developed these solutions to specific problems that large customers faced, the resulting systems were not products yet. They were custom-built, highly integrated, and very expensive platforms, which would later evolve into a viable business for IBM.

These solutions, with all their interconnected hardware and software components, were built as a single system, usually by a small, dedicated team of specialists. Small teams cross-pollinated their expertise so an expert in storage, networks, or databases acquired enough general, working knowledge in other areas. These solutions often required development of new hardware and software technologies, so prolonged cross-pollination of expertise was critical to the success of the project. Team members' close proximity allowed a body of working knowledge to emerge that was critical to the success of the platform. Each team's job was not complete until they delivered a finished, integrated working platform to the customer as a fully functional solution to the business problem.

The End of an Era

In the 1970s, IBM's monopoly was curtailed enough for other startups such as Amdahl, DEC, and Oracle to emerge and begin providing IBM customers with alternatives. DEC built minicomputers that provided superior price/performance to IBM mainframes, but without compatibility. Amdahl (whose namesake, Gene, designed the IBM 390) provided a compatible alternative that was cheaper than an IBM mainframe. Companies could develop and sell their own products or services and thrive in the post-monopoly world.

These pockets of alternative value eventually led to silos of vendors and silos of expertise within IT departments that were aligned with the vendors. Like Amdahl, Oracle directly benefited from technology that IBM developed but never productized. Larry Ellison's genius was to take IBM's relational database technology and place it on the seminal VAX and create one of the first enterprise software companies in the post-mainframe era.

When products within silos or niches were sold to customers, putting the system together was no longer any single supplier's responsibility; it became the customers' job. Today there are so many vendors for every imaginable silo—network switches, storage switches, storage arrays, servers, operating systems, databases, language compilers, applications—and all the complication and cost that comes with the responsibility.

User
Client Application
Browser
Internet
Web Servers
Network
Application Layer
Network
Database
Network
Storage

Watermark of Coherent Persistency

Big systems integrators like Accenture and Wipro attempt to fill this gap, but they also operate within the constraints of IT departments and the same organizational silos established by vendors. Silos are the price paid for the post-mainframe alternatives to IBM. Silos obfuscate the true nature of computing platforms as a single system of interconnected hardware and software.

Back to the Future

Oracle profited from being a post-mainframe silo for decades as customers bought their database technology and ran it on Sun, HP, and EMC hardware. As applications became more complex, constructing platforms with silos became even more difficult. Enterprises attempting to use Oracle's clustering technology, RAC, found it nearly impossible to set up. Since this failure could be a result of their customers' own poor platform engineering (which exposed more bugs), Oracle designed an engineered platform that combined all the components and product engineering expertise, which made successful experiences possible. The resulting product, Exadata, was originally designed for the data warehouse market, but found more success with mainstream Oracle RAC customers running applications like SAP.

Since Oracle was not a hardware company, the initial release of Exadata was based on HP hardware, but Exadata was successful enough that

Oracle decided to source the hardware components themselves, which partially motivated their acquisition of Sun. By sourcing all the hardware and software components in Exadata, Oracle resurrected the one-stop shop mainframe model.

This one-stop shop model is also known as one throat to choke. On its surface, it sounds appealing, but it assumes the throat can be choked. Large customers such as Amgen, Citibank, and AT&T purchase so much equipment and services that they can choke any vendor they like when things go south. However, for the vast majority of customers, because they are too large to manage their own databases without support from Oracle and too small to demand good or timely support from Oracle, one-stop shopping often reduces customers' leverage with vendors.

Like Exadata, big data supercomputers need to be constructed as engineered platforms, and this construction requires an engineering approach where all the hardware and software components are treated as a single system. That's the platform way—the way it was before these components were sold by silos of vendors.

Engineering Big Data Platforms

Big data platforms must operate and process data at a scale that leaves little room for error. Like a Boeing 737, big data clusters must be built for speed, scale, and efficiency. Many enterprises venturing into big data don't have experience building and operating supercomputers, but many are now faced with that prospect. Platform awareness will increase their chances of success with big data.

Thinking about computing systems in a holistic, organic, and integrative way may be considered crazy or not worth the bother; especially when many systems built within organizations seem to operate successfully as silos, just not at peak performance or efficiency. The silo approach achieves operational economies of scale because that is what is being measured. Measuring a platform's efficiency might be almost as hard as building an efficient platform in the first place.

Today, architects who would be responsible for building these new platforms are mostly found in their respective IT departments where they work as subject matter experts in their particular silo. Yet platform architects, like building architects, must have an extensive working knowledge of the entire platform, including the computer science bits, the physical plant aspects, and the business value of the entire platform. Because any component of the platform can be triaged, repaired, or optimized, platform architects must be versed enough to carry on a conversation with data center electricians, network designers, Linux or java programmers, UI designers, and business owners and controllers.

Platform architects must be able and agile enough to dive into the details deep-end with the electrician, and then climb out to dive into another pool full of accountants. Too much knowledge or over-familiarity with details in one area can distort the overall platform perspective. Having the ability to selectively filter out details is required because details come in all shapes and sizes and their relative importance constantly shifts. The cliché "the devil is in the details" is not quite accurate; the devil is usually in a handful of a zillion details and that handful may change daily. Prioritizing the important details and ignoring irrelevant details is one of the most important skills a platform architect can posses.

Designing systems as platforms is a craft not taught, so those who do pick it up stumble on it by accident, necessity, or desperation. This adventure rarely comes with help or encouragement from coworkers, employers, or vendors. It is a thankless learning process that can easily alienate colleagues in other groups because it appears that platform architects are trying to do everybody else's job for them. The truth is that platform architects are trying to a job nobody knows how to do or is willing to do. As a result, most practitioners do not work within IT organizations, but freelance around the rough edges where things don't work, scale, or recover. Freelance platform architects are typically hired to triage problems that have customers at their wit's end. Once fires have been put out, there is a narrow window of opportunity to educate customers about their own platform.

The Art and Craft of Platform Engineering

Platform engineering can be a great, yet hair-raising, adventure. In order to build a platform you have never built before and to discover things that your business never thought to look for, it will take a lot of lab work and many experiments that need to fail early and often to make sure the platform will deliver at scale.

Many enterprise IT departments and their corresponding vendor silos continue to impair platform awareness. Many customers struggle with big data because they want to apply enterprise-grade practices to internet-scale problems. Disaster recovery (DR) is a good example of how the silo perspective rarely produces a strategy that effectively and efficiently recovers a platform. Building a silo-centric DR plan forces precise coordination across every single silo, which is organizationally complex and expensive. When the storage group implements DR strategies, they only do it for storage. When the application server group implements DR, it's limited to the application servers. Although many companies get by with a silo approach to enterprise-scale disaster recovery, it's rarely optimal. At internet-scale, it doesn't work at all.

The tenets of platform engineering apply to both enterprise- and internet-scale computing. The only difference is that at enterprise scale, the mantras are optional. At internet scale, they're mandatory. The art and craft of platform engineering at internet scale demands three critical tenets: avoid complexity, prototype perpetually, and optimize everything.

KISS Me Kate

There are advantages to avoiding complexity at enterprise scale, but at internet scale, "Keep It Simple, Sunshine" are words to live by. Even a modest big data cluster with 20 racks, 400 nodes, and 4,800 disks contains a lot of moving parts and is a complex organism. Complexity contributes to two major failure categories: software bugs and operator error.

Big data platforms must be designed to scale and continue to work in the face of failure. Because the law of averages for a 400-node cluster means failures will inevitably happen, the software must provide the ability to scale and keep the cluster continuously available in the face of component failures. The software supports high availability (HA) by providing both redundancy of service through multiple pathways and self-correcting techniques that reinstates data loss due to failures. In traditional enterprise-scale software, HA capabilities are not valued as features because HA does nothing new or improved–it just keeps things working. But in supercomputer clusters with thousands of interconnected components, HA is as important as scalability.

Historically, HA software features were designed to address hardware failures, but what happens when the HA software fails? Verifying software robustness is a difficult exercise in end-case testing that requires a ruthless and costly devotion to negative testing. And even if vendors are ruthless, the environment they use is rarely end-case identical to their customers' environment. No two platforms are alike unless they are built to extremely repeatable specifications. For this very reason, internet-scale pioneers go to great lengths to minimize platform variance in an attempt to avoid conditions that might trigger end-case, high-complexity software failures, which are very nasty to triage.

Perpetual Prototyping

Product development principles are a bit of a mixed bag and can sometimes backfire. Although it might be noble to preserve design principles that ensure product stability, the price paid for this is a sclerotic software product lifecycle. Many enterprises now find themselves under such immense competitive pressure to add features to their computing plant that traditional approaches to product development might not produce better results than the old approach when IT projects were treated as projects, not products. Rapidly evolving requirements seem to break both the one-off project approach and the bureaucratic software product lifecycle. In this new world, development, testing, and migration all begin to blur together as a single continuous activity.

In the old software development model, there were meetings to discuss the market requirements, and then more meetings to discuss and negotiate the product requirements that would eventually appear in the next release. Finally, the actual development of new features could take years. By the time the features appeared using the old method, competitors using the new approach would have released several versions that were more capable and less stable in the short run, but more capable and stable far faster than with the old model. A long product development cycle can result in an expensive, late, or uncompetitive product. It also can lead to company failure. The traditional process is simply not responsive enough for big data.

Because adding features quickly can destabilize any software system, achieving equilibrium between innovation and stability is important. To shift to a higher rate of release and still provide features that are stable, many internet-scale organizations develop their products using an approach called perpetual prototyping (PP), which blurs together the formerly discrete steps of prototyping, development, testing, and release into a continuous loop. The features are created and delivered so quickly that the released product (or big data platform) is a highly functional prototype.

Companies using a PP style of development have pushed testing and integration phases into sections of their production environment. Their production environments (aka colos) are so vast that it is more cost effective to use a small slice of users spread across the entire set of colos than it is to construct a separate test colo. This users-as-guinea-pigs model can obviously have negative effects on any users who are subjected to untested code, but the simulation is extremely realistic, and steps are taken to make sure the new features are not so broken that it creates havoc.

The open source world has strategies that are similar to PP, where early versions of code are pushed out to users with "tech preview" status. In addition to branches that barely compile, as well as more stable production versions, tech preview operates like a warning label: it should work as advertised; if it doesn't, give us a shout. This code might even be production-ready, but it has had limited exposure to production environments.

Relative to traditional methods, open source development also trades rapid evolution (feature time to market) for stability. In early stages of development, the product improves quickly, but with quality sometimes going sideways more often than in a traditional closed-source model. As products or projects stabilize and fewer features are added, developers lose interest and work on the next shiny bright thing and the rate of change drops off. Even open source products eventually stop changing or become stable enough that the loss of these developers is really a sign of maturity.

Optimize Everything at Internet Scale

Internet-scale platforms must operate at such a high level of performance, complexity, and cost that their solution space must always be optimized at the intersection of operations, economics, and architecture. These three dimensions are fundamental to any form of platform design, whether the platform is a supercomputer cluster or a Honda Civic. Platforms can still be successful without being optimized in all dimensions, but the more optimized, the more efficient. Determining whether a platform is as optimized as it should be is as difficult and subjective as designing the platform in the first place. Enterprises that want to fully realize the benefits of big data will also find themselves with internet-scale expectations of their platforms, staff, and vendors.

Big data platforms are monster computers. A single Hadoop cluster with serious punch consists of hundreds of racks of servers and switches. These racks do not include the surrounding infrastructure used to get the bales of data onto the cluster. Many enterprises can set up hundreds of racks of gear, but few can stand them up as a single supercomputing platform. Getting a Hadoop cluster up and running is hard enough, but optimizing it in all dimensions is a whole other pool of fish. Optimization is about maximizing productivity and making the most of your precious resources, whether they are myelin, metal, or baked from sand.

Optimizing a platform means spending money more wisely, not just spending less on what might appear to be the same value. Any organization can reduce costs by not spending money, but that's not optimization—that's just spending less money while assuming that quality remains constant; as if laying off employees never affects the remaining staff. These kinds of "productivity improvements" are often misconstrued as optimization. Cutting costs always makes a business more profitable, but not necessarily more efficient or strategically positioned.

Every part of a platform that contributes to economic activity can be optimized and all forms of activity have value or utility. "Bang for the buck" is another way to say optimize everything; the bang comes from anywhere, anything, or anyone. It can mean either spending fewer bucks for a given bang, or squeezing more bang from a single buck. A simple optimization strategy for data circuits running between Texas and Montana could include improving the software engineering used to route data, or buying a cheaper set of switches that provide just the required capabilities, or renegotiating service level agreements with the carrier. The strategy to optimize everything is an operational example of perpetual prototyping.

The Response Time Continuum

High availability (HA) has mostly been concerned with avoiding outages. When customers book an airline reservation, the entire platform must be available and responsive to make this possible. When parts of a platform are not available (like the reservation database), another copy of the database must be brought online so customers can continue to book flights. Database teams pride themselves on designing disaster recovery strategies that make this continued availability possible, but if the rest of the platform isn't designed to the same level of availability, the customer experience suffers. HA isn't just about keeping databases or storage up and running; it's about keeping everything up and running, from the user's browser to the air conditioners in the datacenter.

Engineering for high availability is not just about avoiding long outages—it is about any outage, even the ones that last just a few seconds. When customers are waiting for the platform to return a selection of airline flights that match their search criteria, a few seconds of unavailability in the reservation system might as well be forever, especially if their reservation is lost. Availability is about the responsiveness of the system, so the response time continuum encompasses the seconds or minutes customers must wait for their reservation to complete as well as the hours or days it might take the system to recover from a major disaster.

The responsiveness and degree of unavailability is determined both by expectations and the perception of time. Some online systems display messages (don't move away from this screen until your reservation is complete) or dials (working…working…working…) to manage users' expectations of responsiveness. It might be OK with customers to wait a minute or two longer to ensure that their airline tickets are booked correctly and paid for only once, but currency traders feel that a wait of 500 milliseconds is unbearable. Performance, scalability, and recovery have always been perceived as separate topics of platform design, but they're all just sub-topics of availability engineering.

The Availability Spectrum

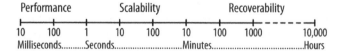

Epic Fail Insurance

Design doctrines for enterprise-grade platforms are based on established principles that make sense for critical enterprise-scale computing systems, such as payroll. To be considered enterprise-grade, many people think big data must embrace enterprise-scale doctrines. But enterprise-grade doctrines are neither affordable nor designed for use at internet scale. Enterprise big data requires a new category that combines the robustness of enterprise-grade practice with internet-scale affordability.

A good example is the system redundancy strategy of no single point of failure (noSPOF). System redundancy is a design principle applied to platforms to allow them to function in the presence of abnormal operating conditions. For example, in the past, Ethernet hardware interfaces used to be so unreliable they needed protection through redundancy. As those parts became integrated into servers, their reliability improved to the point where the software protecting against their failure was less reliable than the hardware it was designed to protect. At enterprise scale, it is often easy to implement the noSPOF policy because the cost and complexity are tolerable. At internet scale, HA for computing platforms that often span multiple datacenters requires more affordable strategies.

At internet scale, not all single points of failure are created equal, so applying the principle across all potential points of failure is difficult to implement, complex to manage, and very expensive. The top three categories of system failure are physical plant, operator error, and software bugs. In an attempt to reduce failures, the noSPOF policy becomes overused, which introduces so much complexity that it ends up reducing reliability. At internet scale, these negative effects are greatly magnified. Enterprise-scale systems are typically not highly distributed and are more susceptible to just a few critical pathways of failure. Internet-scale distributed systems also contain critical pathways, but have fewer of them in addition to having many parallel service pathways.

All systems contain critical pathways, which if they fail, would create some form of unavailability. When trying to figure out which points of failure are critical, the first question is often "what happens if it fails?" but the more important question is "what happens when it fails?" The first question assumes deterministic failure and is often expressed as Murphy's Law: if it can fail, it will. In reality, everything doesn't fail. There are parts that *might* fail but not all parts *do* fail, so it is important to assess the probability of a part failing. The next question to ask is "what is the outcome of the failure"?

A critical pathway is defined both by its probability of occurring and its severity of outcome. They all have a pathway severity index (PSI), which is a combination of the probability and outcome (or reduction in availability) from the failure of each pathway. Any pathway—whether in hardware or software—with a high PSI requires a redundancy strategy. The noSPOF strategy is overused at enterprise-scale because it is often easier to apply it everywhere than it is to determine which pathways have a high severity index.

The strategy of over-deploying noSPOF compromises reliability because the complexity ends up increasing the PSI for the pathway. Distributed systems have many more pathways, which spread out and reduce the risk of critical pathway failures that could result in complete platform failure. Because internet-scale platforms are highly distributed, the effect of the distribution replaces just a few high PSI pathways with hundreds of low PSI pathways. And low PSI pathways do not require noSPOF. At either enterprise or internet scale, rough estimates of PSI can help prioritize where redundancy bets should be placed. Locating aspects of design within the gap between recklessness and risk aversion will result in a more optimized platform.

The noSPOF doctrine is enterprise-scale availability engineering. The internet-scale version must be solved and optimized within the economic, architectural, and operational dimensions that constrain any platform. Avoiding epic failure at internet scale mandates the need to understand how distributed systems optimize for availability by keeping it simple and keeping it easy because that keeps it reliable.

Mind the Gap

In order to optimize aspects of any business, more accurate risk analysis is required. And in order to optimize aspects of any platform, more accurate risk analysis is required. There is a continuum of risk between aversion and recklessness. Some businesses can afford to be risk averse, but most cannot. To mitigate risk, corporations employ many strategies that require some degree of calculated risk. Sometimes it is calculated very accurately with numbers and sometimes employees just have to make educated guesses.

In preparation for big data, corporations need to optimize some of the computing systems that are now the heart and lungs of their business. Accurately analyzing the risk of component failure within any platform (hardware, software, humans, or competitors) is a key to optimizing the efficiency of those platforms. It might seem odd to consider the competitive landscape or a group of employees to be platforms, but all behave like interconnected systems.

I'll Take Silos for $1000, Alex

One of the surprises awaiting enterprises is that big data is DIY supercomputing. Whatever big data cluster they stand up, it comes from the factory without applications or data. In order to populate the cluster, data must be emancipated from their own technical and organizational silos. Big data matters because of the business value it promises. Data scientists and data wranglers will need to develop new methods to analyze both the legacy data and the vast amounts of new data flooding in. Both Development and Operations will be responsible for the success of an enterprise's big data initiative. The walls between the business, data, organizations, and platform cannot exist at internet scale.

Similar to your nervous system, a big data cluster is a highly interconnected platform built from a collection of commodity parts. Neurons in the human brain are the building blocks of the nervous system, but are very simple parts. The neurons in a jellyfish are also made from these very simple parts. Just like you are far more than the sum of your jellyfish parts (your brilliant personality being the nervous system's ultimate big data job), a big data cluster operates as a complex, interconnected form of computing intelligence—almost human, almost Watson.

CHAPTER 3

Organizations: The Other Platform

From Myelin to Metal

The world of advanced big data platforms is a strange place. Like a Gilbert and Sullivan musical, there is drama, farce, and mayhem in every act. Once in a long while, the curtain rises, time stands still, and as if by magic, it all works. Platform engineering at internet scale is an art form—a delicate balance of craft, money, personalities, and politics. With the commoditization of IT, however, there is much less craft and little art. Studies have shown that 60 to 80 percent of all IT projects fail with billions of dollars wasted annually. The end results are not simply inefficient, but frequently unusable. Projects that do finish are often late, over budget, or missing most of their requirements.

There is immense pressure on CIOs to convert their IT infrastructure into something as commodity as the plumbing in their office buildings. Deploying platforms on the scale required for cloud computing or big data will be the most complex projects IT groups undertake. Managing complex projects of this magnitude requires a healthy IT culture not only to ensure the successful discovery of the insights the business craves, but to continuously deliver those insights in a cost-effective way. Computing platforms deeply impact the corporation they serve, not to mention the end users, vendors, partners, and shareholders. This mobius strip of humanity and technology lies at the heart of the very model of a modern major enterprise. A socially productive IT organization is a prerequisite for success with big data.

Humans organized themselves into hierarchies well before the water cooler appeared. In a corporate organization, hierarchies try to balance the specialization of labor and details only specialists worry about by distilling minutiae so that leaders can make informed business decisions without being confused or overwhelmed. Distilling minutiae relies on preserving the right amount of detail and abstracting the rest. Because details are not created equal, the goal of abstraction is to prioritize the right details and mask the ones that cause confusion and fear, both of which do a cracker jack job of impairing judgment. When done well, a lot of good decisions can be made very quickly and course corrections sometimes can make up for bad decisions. Since organizations are made up of people whose motivation, emotions, and behavior combine with their understanding of topics to produce those judgments, it is rarely done well, let alone efficiently.

Silos

In large organizations, at the expense of having generalists organized around the platform, IT departments are set up as hierarchies of specialization to achieve economies of scale. Silos are a result of hierarchies, which need to organize people into economically effective groups. In IT, these silos are groups of specialists. A group of database administrators (DBAs) are specialists who scale more economically when their group must grow from supporting tens to hundreds of databases. DBAs are specialists in databases, but not in storage. Storage Admins are specialists with spindles, but inexperienced at tuning SQL queries. However, fixing poor platform performance often requires actual collaborative work among specialties, and merely attending meetings together doesn't cut it.

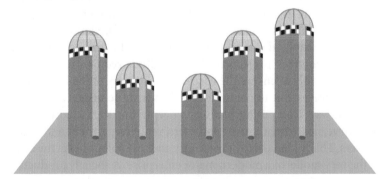

Smaller silos within silos often emerge in large corporations; for example, storage administration and database administration are typically collected together in the Operations silo, whereas UI design and application programming are contained in the Development silo. If it's politically difficult for DBAs to communicate with Storage Admins, then DBAs and UI designers are barely aware of each other's existence.

Although enterprises like to organize employees into silos and sub-silos, the platform is not well served, and whenever the platform fails to scale, recover, or accommodate new business, each silo is potentially implicated. All computing platforms span horizontally across organizations from the physical plant all the way out to the firewall. Big data platforms also span horizontally, but they are even more extreme—technically, financially, and politically. The silo structure is not well suited for developing and managing platforms at internet scale.

Though they have administrative and economic value, silos suppress cross-functional awareness and discourage generalists with a working knowledge of the platform who could fill a very important technical and diplomatic role. Some organizations have an Infrastructure or Reference Architecture group populated by individuals who seem to be the stewards of the platform. Both technical and non-technical expertise must be represented in this group for the platform to be properly represented; instead, it's often staffed with experienced technical experts with deep expertise in a limited area of the platform and frequently reports into Operations with little representation from Development, Marketing, or Finance. If the infrastructure group is given the authority to behave unilaterally, it compromises the diplomatic mission. There is always a fine line between diplomacy, moral suasion, and unilateralism. Done well, this group serves both the platform and business. Done poorly, this group ends up being just another silo.

Other companies construct "tiger teams" by forcing subject matter experts from a number of different silos to work together temporarily. In contrast, when teams of specialists in the '50s and '60s needed to develop a working knowledge of those old mainframe systems, they were given the latitude and time to cross-pollinate their skills as specialists in one area and generalists in others. Never a part-time job, specialists learning to be working generalists must be given the time to understand the rest of the platform. Not all specialists will be comfortable or adept at cultivating breadth of knowledge, so the casting of tiger teams is extremely critical. Tiger teams fail when members are miscast or never allowed to forget which silo they really work for.

Industrial Grain Elevators

If it's hard for IT departments to tear down silos, imagine how hard it will be for the industry. Silos partially arose from the ashes of the one-stop-shop, single-vendor mainframe model. Vendors specializing in network or storage products found it easier to sell to network or storage groups and so reinforced the emerging silos of specialization. The products from these companies were optimized for the specific demographics of specialists, so they evolved away from a platform awareness and closer to the particular needs of each silo of subject matter expertise. Poor interoperability of multiple vendors' products is the best example of this force in action and over time the platform became obfuscated.

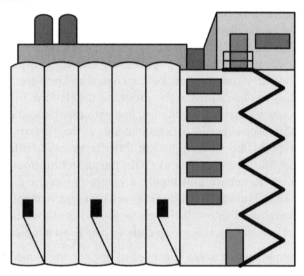

Some vendors are attempting a revival of the one-stop approach—mostly to increase the growth of their business, not necessarily to benefit the platform, their customers, or big data. But customers have distant (or recent, if they own the odd PC) memories of one-stop that may not be all that pleasant. Throat choking is harder than it looks and, on closer inspection, the current one-stop attempts by larger vendors can't tear down their own internal silos (oddly enough, vendors have organizations, too). They end up operating as several competing businesses under one brand.

Vendors who are now attempting one-stop shops still prefer the silo model, especially if they have franchise strength. Vendors who aspire to use big data to grow their current portfolio of products certainly don't want to sacrifice their existing revenue base. For some vendors, it will be a zero sum game. For others, it will be far less than zero because the economic rules of the big data ecosystem are unlike the economic rules of the current enterprise ecosystem. Like Kodak, whose business and margins were based on film not memories, traditional enterprise vendors will need to base their big data offerings on insight, not on capture or strand.

In the past decade, customers have grown increasingly dependent on advice from vendors. The codependency between vendors and IT departments is a well-entrenched, natural consequence of silos. It is now difficult for IT groups to be informed consumers, and the commoditization of staff has not helped. Drained of advanced engineering talent, IT has outsourced this expertise to service companies or even vendors. For example, when enterprises take advice on how to do disaster recovery from their storage and database vendors, they get completely different answers. Vendors always try to convince customers that their silo-centric solution is superior; however, vendors don't always have their customers' best interests in mind.

Like performance and scalability, disaster recovery is one of the tougher problems in platform engineering. Even with the benefit of a platform perspective, doing DR well requires a delicate balance of speed, budget, and a good set of dice. Attempting it from within silos is far more painful, since silo-centric solutions are usually about how to avoid being implicated in the event of an actual disaster. Most solutions consist of a piecemeal strategy cobbled together from competing vendors. Once again, the platform takes it on the chin.

Platforms 1, Silos 0

The plethora of intertwined software and hardware that are part of a platform stubbornly refuse to operate like a dozen independent silos. Disaster recovery and performance problems are tough to triage even with a modest enterprise platform, but they take on a degree of complexity that is exponential in a 400-node cluster. Commercial supercomputers must transcend both the mechanics and politics of silos to be successful.

When performance problems are triaged within silos, the result is often like a game of schoolyard tag. The group with the most glaring symptoms gets tagged. If that's storage, then the admins must either find and fix the storage problem or "prove" that it wasn't their fault. The storage group rarely understands application code and they are not encouraged to cross-pollinate with application developers. Likewise, many developers are far removed from the physical reality of the platform underneath them and they have no incentive to understand what happens to the platform when they add a seemingly insignificant feature that results in an extra 300,000 disk reads. Whenever something goes seriously wrong within a computing platform, the organization of silos demands accountability. There are usually a couple of platform-aware individuals lurking within IT departments; they're the ones who determine that the "insignificant" feature caused the "storage" performance problem. The good news for each silo is that it's not just their fault. The bad news is that often it's everyone's fault.

Advances such as Java and hypervisors and a general reliance on treating the computing platform in abstract terms have reinforced the notion that it is no longer necessary to understand how computers actually work. Big data is about performance and scalability first, so knowing what the hardware is doing with the software will become important again.

Panic! Now!

When everything is working as planned and being delivered on time within budget, silos of specialists are economical and make sense to the organization. When platforms fail and the underlying problem is masked by silos, statements like "perception is reality" start to swirl around the water cooler. If you hear this enough where you work, you should start to move toward higher ground. As various groups scramble to make sure the problem is not theirs, the combination of fear and ignorance starts to set in and results in impaired judgment or panic.

Silos must compete for budgets, up-time stats, and political credibility, which frequently leaves the platform and business undefended. When the organization is more important than the business, companies can become their own worst enemy.

Fear and Loathing

Organizations of any size are comprised of humans who all have varying tolerances for fear and risk. In order to make good judgments, our brains must discern and sort complex and competing bits of information. Fear does weird things to the human brain by disrupting its ability to make good judgments. The impairment from this disruption can lead to dysfunctional behavior. But we are not robots; making decisions without any emotion at all is considered a psychological disorder. Studies have shown that every single decision has an emotional component, no matter how insignificant. Research subjects with these pathways fully disrupted find it difficult to even choose what cereal to have for breakfast. Decision-making is a delicate balance of signals between the emotional part of the brain (amygdala) and the thinking part (ventromedial prefrontal cortex).

What does good judgment have to do with big data? Everything. For organizations amped on ego and ambition, combined with the intolerance for error that comes with the complexity and scale of big data, this means a lot of decisions will have to be made quickly and without all the information. And that requires judgment.

Fear and anger are two sides of the same impairment coin. The emotional, primitive part of the brain is responsible for fight or flight. Fear is flight, anger is fight—both are good at impairing judgment. For example, if I'm meeting with someone whom I've clashed with on a previous project, my emotional perception of their opinion will be distorted by my feelings toward them. I might unconsciously misinterpret what they are saying due to body language, tone of voice, or choice of words—all of which communicate information. Also, as I listen for subtext, plot their downfall, or construct a whole new conspiracy theory, I might not be really listening to them at all.

Making good decisions isn't just about *not* being emotionally impaired by fear or anger. It also isn't about knowing *all* the details, but about prioritizing just the right few. Since there are always too many details, the human brain must learn how to find those few that matter. Finding them requires our old reptile and new mammal brains to dance; fear and anger definitely kill the music.

A business relies on its staff to sort and prioritize details every day. Experience and informed judgment is required. It's called business acumen or an educated guess. When you guess right, you are a hero; when you guess wrong, that's OK—you just need to guess again, often with no new information, but mistakes are how humans learn. Big data is a new, completely uncharted world with problems that have never been encountered. Right or wrong, those who guess faster will learn faster. Prepare to make a lot of mistakes and learn at lot.

Risky Business

Small companies have a cultural acceptance for risk that gets diluted as the company grows. Small companies may appear reckless when viewed from the risk-averse end of the spectrum where large companies operate; an acceptance for taking calculated risks is not reckless. Risk aversion often seems safe (better safe than sorry), but you can be sorry if you are too safe.

Every year, surfers from all over the world attempt to surf 20-story waves off the coast of Northern California at Maverick's. From the viewpoint of risk aversion, these surfers seem like lunatics. Because a reckless surfer is a dead surfer, surfers must be effective risk technicians. Similarly, rock climbers on the face of El Capitan in Yosemite National Park, especially the free climb variety, are also considered lunatics. In exchange for determining risks, which involves invaluable intuition and years of experience, surfers and climbers are rewarded with exhilarating experiences.

An organization's operating risk spectrum is the gap between aversion and recklessness. In business, being risk averse is more about perception of risk than actual risk, so the gap between aversion and recklessness often contains competitors who are willing to take on more risk. If you don't believe there is a large gap, then you might be complacent about the competition, but the gap can be wide enough to accommodate both competitors and opportunities for new business. Disruptive forces like big data also widen the gap, and accurately perceiving this gap relies heavily on how well your old and new brains can get along. Making better decisions requires us to become better at accurately assessing risk.

Probability and Outcome

Probability is an idea; outcome is an experience. Humans tend to perceive risk based on outcome rather than probability. Like most mathematics, probability is based on how the natural world functions at an empirical level and probability is an idea, whereas outcome is grounded in experience. Using the classic case of driving versus flying, although we know it's far riskier to drive down US Interstate 5 than to catch the shuttle to Burbank, this doesn't wash with the human psyche. If a plane crashes, the subsequent outcome of something very bad happening (i.e., death) is almost certain. However, the probability of being killed in a car crash is less certain than taking that commuter flight. You have a better chance of surviving the outcome, so it seems less risky. Severity of outcome has no bearing on the probability of the accident in the first place, but this is how our brains work. Good risk technicians must fight this instinct in order to do things mere mortals would never dream of—surf the waves at Maverick's or surf the capital burndown of a startup that takes on IBM.

Deterministic risk analysis is another example of aversion. In an attempt to protect the business from all *possible* outcomes, instead of all *probable* outcomes, organizations often assume the worst. They assume that failures will occur. Deterministic analysis assumes that all possible failures will happen; probabilistic analysis assumes the components that are most likely to fail are the ones that actually fail. Being a better risk technician will help to optimize the platform.

Quantitative Qualities

One sure-fire way to get accountants and controllers mad at you is to ask them to quantify qualitative risk. Turns out, although this is not happening in spreadsheets, it's happening at an intuitive level all the time in the form of the thousands of business decisions made every day. An easy example of qualitative risk analysis is found when making a decision about recruiting new employees. The decision to hire one candidate over another, though a subjective judgment, involves the brain doing what it does well: making decisions with qualitative information.

There is nothing mathematical about intuition; so it's an unmentionable word in many organizations. Not because it isn't used everyday to make decisions, but because it appears to be biased or non-linear or random. Good intuition is far from random and can allow for very quick decision making. Having the patience to listen for and recognize good intuition in others makes it possible for people to make better decisions faster.

The Soft Platform

Organizations don't kill projects; people kill projects, and sometimes projects kill people. All are bad clichés, but it seems that some organizations have become bad clichés, too. Getting humans to work as a well-oiled machine is the hardest part of the soft platform—hard to understand, hard to preserve the innovation, and hard to change.

Changes in organizational behavior happen at a glacial rate relative to the technology and business conditions that accompany trends like big data. Humans simply can't change their patterns of behavior fast enough to keep up with technological advances. It's a cultural impedance mismatch. The rate of acceptance of big data—which came up quickly on the heels of the cloud computing craze—will be necessarily slow and erratic. "We just figured out clouds, and now you want us to do what?"

Big data also brings with it a shift in the demographics of professionals as open source programmers and data scientists bring energy and new approaches to an established industry. Anthropology and technology are converging to produce a major shift in how everyone consumes data—enterprises, customers, agencies, and even the researchers studying how humans behave in organizations.

CHAPTER 4

The Reservoir of Data

The Actual Internet

We wouldn't be talking about big data at all if it weren't for the "explosion" of the internet. Several technologies that were drifting around in the 1980s eventually converged to make the first boom possible. Mainstream consumer culture experienced it as if the boom came from nowhere. Since the 1990s, the internet has taken a few more evolutionary steps. Running a business or computing plant at internet scale had never been done before Yahoo! and then Google and Facebook attempted it. They solved many engineering problems that arose while taking commercial supercomputing from enterprise scale to internet scale. But as Yahoo! has since demonstrated, making a sustainably profitable business out of internet-scale computing is a different matter.

Traditional enterprises (companies that make films, 737s, or soap) are for the first time experiencing internet-scale computing problems, but they're still stuck with their decades-old, entrenched approach to enterprise-scale computing. For those who remember what happened in the 1990s—or, more to the point, what didn't happen—skepticism about the Miracle of Big Data is justified. Taken from the perspective that early technologies (for example, Java, Apache, or anything involving billions of users) are always unproven, the first boom is always going to be wishful thinking. And there was a lot of wishful thinking going on in the 1990s.

Many startup companies built prototypes using early technologies like the programming language Java, which made it easier to quickly develop applications. If a startup's idea caught on, then the problem of too many customers quickly overwhelmed the designers' intentions. Good problem to have. Building platforms to scale requires a lot of scaffolding "tax" up front, and although a startup might wish for too many customers, building a system from the get-go to handle millions of customers was expensive, complex, and optimistic even for Silicon Valley startups in the 1990s.

An application could be designed to quickly demonstrate that pet food could be purchased online, but demonstrating this for millions of pet owners would require the annoying platform-engineering bits to work, which rarely came into question during angel, seed, or mezzanine phases of funding. Startups with a good idea and a reasonable application could soon be crushed by their inability to scale. Companies trying to design a killer app would be pressured to constantly tweak the design in an attempt to land millions of customers in one quarter. Core design requirements could reverse every few weeks, and this redesign whirlpool became inescapable. Very few companies survived.

Amazon is often cited as a survivor, and many of the original core architects who built Amazon came from Wal-Mart, which had built one of the first at-scale inventory management platforms on the planet. Wal-Mart did such an impressive job that they changed forever the rules of supply chains, inventory, and retail. Startup companies that did not acquire a modest amount of platform engineering chops or could not constrain their instinct to "add one more thing" did not survive, despite having a viable business plan and several hundred thousand customers.

Best of Inbred

Platform engineering embodies the mantra "the whole is more than the sum of its parts" and can make up for many deficiencies in particular technologies. Components of a platform do not have to be mature or stable—that is the best-of-breed myth corresponding to the current silo view of enterprise engineering. A best-of-breed platform does not require all components to be best of breed, nor will a platform assembled from best-of-breed technology necessarily be best of breed either. Best of breed is a concept introduced by the enterprise silo vendors; it's often the product with the most brand strength in a given silo.

Best of breed is simply unaffordable at internet scale. Building successful platforms can be done with a broader pedigree among components because the pedigree is dictated by scalability and affordability. If architects can make a data center full of noSQL database engines meet the business requirements, then they can get by without the sophistication and expense of Oracle. This doesn't mean MySQL can replace Oracle or that surgically deploying DB2 is off the table either. But if the platform needs to handle hundreds of millions of users affordably, the secret sauce is in the platform engineering, not in the aggregation of best-of-breed products.

Some enterprises have been living with and managing their big data for a long time. Healthcare companies have been trying to archive patient histories since they built their earliest databases. Some of these records live on legacy arrays and some are hibernating on tape reels. In order to discover insights from legacy data, it must be accessible. Moving that data into a shiny new Hadoop cluster will require solving several platform-engineering problems that will make standing up that shiny new object look easy.

There's so much pent up demand for big data because companies have been trying to do it for 20 years, but vendors couldn't offer solutions that were affordable at scale. And because data lives everywhere, no single product or suite of products from any given vendor can really "solve" big data problems. Even enterprises that attempted the one-stop-shop approach over the last decade have ended up with several, if not many, isolated or stranded sources of data. Customers now have sources stranded on Greenplum, Netezza, and Exadata, and they risk stranding new sources on Cassandra, Mongo, and even Hadoop.

Like scientific supercomputing, commercial supercomputing cannot be solved using products from a single vendor. Big data consists of a broad spectrum of purpose-built workloads, but traditional business intelligence products are either too general-purpose to address this diverse spectrum or too purpose-built and can only address a narrow range of workloads. Big data requires a strange, new hybrid platform-product, but this will give software vendors fits because a well-designed, heterogeneous product that can be form-fitted to each enterprise's very peculiar mosh pit of old and new data makes for a lousy SKU and a complicated story. Vendors don't like complicated stories.

Drowning Not Waving

By the time you read this, big data may already be a cliché or routinely parodied on YouTube. For many enterprises, big data was a cruel and expensive joke 20 years ago. The data warehousing products created in the 1990s were outgrowths of major RDBMS vendors who got an early glimpse of the tsunami. This first-generation technology was made possible due to advances in server technology. Hardware companies like DEC, HP, and IBM (prodded by startups like Pyramid, Sequent, and SGI) designed servers that were finally powerful enough to execute queries against a terabyte of data.

A small startup, Teradata, developed one of the first database kernels to handle queries against a TB of data. Established database companies like Informix, Oracle, and Sybase were soon chasing Teradata. Vendors who had spent years building kernels that were optimized for transaction processing needed to re-tool their kernels in order to handle queries that could process a thousand times as much data.

Some companies developed purpose-built kernels to handle a specific class of workloads (which was the point in time where big data really started). This early, difficult, clumsy, and expensive market has been called a lot of things over the years—decision support, OLAP, data warehouse, business intelligence (BI)—but even in the 1990s, it was important enough that the benchmark standards committee, TPC, defined a benchmark to help users qualify industry solutions.

To the extent that benchmarks ever help customers make purchasing decisions, these artificial workloads defined a generation of technology and capabilities. As successful as Teradata was at setting the bar for warehouse performance, it turned out to be a mom-and-pop, purpose-built business just like scientific supercomputing. After almost 20 years, Teradata is still a David against the Goliaths of IBM, Oracle, and EMC.

In commercial computing, the highly un-sexy applications for bookkeeping and widget tracking are where the money has always been. Yet, even the Goliaths will have difficulty dominating big data and high performance commercial computing for all the reasons scientific computing was never much of a growth business: purpose-built complex engineering, boutique revenues, and very pregnant sales cycles. Big data is moving so fast relative to the clumsy old industry that standards bodies will find it difficult to define a general-purpose benchmark for a purpose-built world.

As soon as it was possible to extract, transform, and load (ETL) warehouse quantities of data, enterprises started drowning in it. Prior to the 1990s, data sources were abundant, but the high cost of storage still meant stashing much of it on tape. Tape technology has more lives than cats. The simple reason tape is still viable today is due to its economics. Even as disk storage approaches $1/TB, tape remains a couple of orders of magnitude cheaper. Big data starts to live up to its name not when enterprises have 10 petabytes in their cluster, but when they can afford to load 500 exabytes. In that world, tape will still be alive and well because the sensors from which the 500 exabytes originated will be producing 500 zettabytes/year.

Spinning Rust

Hennessey and Paterson have shown that processing technology has more or less tracked Moore's Law, but memory and storage have not. In the early 2000s, the cost of memory started to fall in line with Moore's Law since memory is a semiconductor, but storage technology remained mechanical. The technology of disk drives today is not far removed from disk drives made in the 1980s. The landmark IBM Winchester was made from spinning platters of rust (oxidized particles) and flying magnetic heads, which is still true today for the drives found in a Hadoop cluster.

The recent emergence of flash as storage technology and Hadoop as a low-cost alternative to arrays of expensive disks will combine to produce its own form of disruption to that industry. A flash-based Hadoop cluster, for the first time, will be able to operate on a working set of problems at memory speeds. However, the economics of storing hundreds of petabytes will insure both forms of spinning and spooling rust will be required by big data.

A Spectrum of Perishability

In the old silo world, enterprise data was mission critical, extremely valuable, and should never be lost, corrupted, or compromised. Most enterprise vendors have designed their products to be extremely persistent and in some cases, as with databases, coherently persistent. Today in the land that is flooded with too much data, not only is it too expensive to cherish every bit, it is often not necessary. For the first time, enterprises can afford to crunch on an absurd amount of data for analysis, discovery, and insight. The price of admission is being able to stage 25 PB long enough for the crunch to occur. In many cases, even at $1/TB, keeping 25 PB around after the crunch will be impractical and some data must be tossed. When petabytes become exabytes, exabytes become zettabytes, and zettabytes become yottabytes, then keeping tons of data after it has been crunched will not be an option.

Data lives on a spectrum of perishability that spans from seconds to decades. Data can be so transient that if analysis does not complete within an hour, the shelf life of the insight expires and the data must be deleted to make room for the next hour's data. Perishability puts the emphasis on insight, not retention. Historically, most enterprises have chosen to keep data for as long as possible and as cheaply as possible, but for big data, ideas and policies regarding the duration and cost of retention must be revaluated. Everything lives on a spectrum of perishability: data, technology, and the business itself. Innovation drives the rapid expiration of all three.

Software vendors built warehouse products to run on dedicated hardware out of necessity to ensure their complex product would even work. If the vendor was IBM, these products typically ran on IBM hardware. If the vendor was Oracle, these products typically ran on hardware from one of Oracle's hardware partners such as Dell, HP, or even IBM. Prescribing and packaging the hardware platform increased the odds of a successful deployment.

This trend in engineered systems looks like a platform-aware evolution, but it turns out to be more about vendor franchise management and less about the customer experience. Plus it increases the likelihood of stranding customers' data. Stranded, captive data is the result of vendors optimizing their products for margins and not markets. This approach to product development also tends to stifle innovation. If a franchise remains strong and can be enforced so captives can't escape, vendors can still make a decent living. But no such franchise exists today in big data, even among established players like IBM, Oracle, and EMC.

Enterprise customers continue to purchase new warehouse products that promise to solve all their data problems only to have to move—yet again—all the data from the last failed platform to the new and improved one. Improvements in cost and scale mean that the latest and most capable system ends up with the most data. All of the old platforms did such a good job of snaring data that it became technically or politically difficult (usually both) to migrate to a new system. Many enterprises have an large collection of stranded data sources—not just in last year's database on expensive storage arrays—but vast repositories of analog data (such as X-rays) that haven't yet made it onto that cockroach of all storage mediums, tape.

Enclosed Water Towers

As the tsunami of data inundates enterprises, some may feel that their existing water towers of data are clean and safe from contamination. Despite those tanks being well built and expensive, relative to the millions of gallons of water that come ashore with just the first wave, they hold little and reveal less. The volume of data already coming into enterprises is enough to fill a Los Angeles County service reservoir in minutes. Because enterprises have spent the last 20 years constructing larger and larger water tanks of stranded, captive data, they need to start building reservoirs to safely capture the raw data (including all the debris) so that it can be processed and treated.

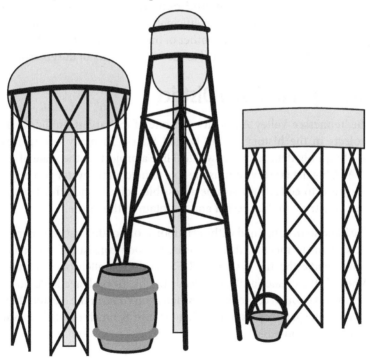

An Oracle database running on EMC hardware is a very capable water tank, but it remains a closed source for only a few analytic residents. For enterprises to reap the benefits that will come from being able to analyze all their aggregated data, both old and new, they must stop stranding data in tanks and start constructing a more open and common reservoir for data that uncouples accessibility from analysis. These new repositories will function like the fresh water reservoirs that serve a city the size of Los Angeles.

In California, the majority of rain falls between November and March, but water demand is constant. Reservoirs are an efficient way to store hundreds of thousands of acre-feet, so water districts use their plumbing and pumps to deliver water to downstream customers. Like water in a tsunami wall or behind an earthen damn that has just failed, water can be an extremely destructive force of nature. Too little water and mammals like you and I end up at the wrong end of our own perishability scale. At rest, too much water is not usually considered a hazard, but water under the influence of gravity or seismicity can get out of control and cause limitless destruction.

Data, like water, must be treated with respect. Mammals need fresh and clean drinking water; enterprises need safe and clean data. Since a big data reservoir will need to efficiently accommodate hundreds of exabytes, it will be worth the bother of building accessible and robust reservoirs. And it will be critical to the sustainability of the enterprise.

The Big Data Water District

The Tennessee Valley Authority was one of the largest public works projects in the history of the United States. To many enterprises, building a big data reservoir will feel like a project on the scale of the TVA. A big data reservoir must be able to hold all the water you might ever need to collect, yet still be accessible, robust, and affordable to both construct in the present and maintain in the future.

The file system contained within Hadoop is one of the first commercial file systems to meet all these criteria. Hadoop consists of two major components: the file system (HDFS) and a parallel job scheduler. When HDFS creates a file, it spreads the file over all available nodes and makes enough copies so that when a job runs on the cluster, there are enough spare copies of the file to insure as much parallelism and protection as possible.

File systems have always been closely associated with databases and operating systems. A file system isn't usually thought of as a distinct piece of technology, but more as a tightly integrated piece or natural extension of the database or operating system kernel. For example, Oracle's database kernel always had aspects of a file system built into it: tables, segments, and extents all perform functions that are associated with a traditional file system.

Veritas was one of the first companies to demonstrate that a file system was valuable enough to stand on its own as a product and didn't have to be embedded within either the OS or database. Veritas is no longer around, but it wasn't because the functional autonomy of a file system was a bad idea. Execution, competitors' egos, and sheer luck influence the destiny of most commercial technologies.

The HDFS Reservoir

The Hadoop Distributed File System is not a complex, feature-rich, kitchen sink file system, but it does two things very well: it's economical and functional at enormous scale. Affordable. At. Scale. Maybe that's all it should be. A big data reservoir should make it possible for traditional database products to directly access HDFS and still provide a canal for enterprises to channel their old data sources into the new reservoir.

Big data reservoirs must allow old and new data to coexist and intermingle. For example, DB2 currently supports table spaces on traditional OS file systems, but when it supports HDFS directly, it could provide customers with a built-in channel from the past to the future. HDFS contains a feature called federation that, over time, could be used to create a reservoir of reservoirs, which will make it possible to create planetary file systems that can act locally but think globally.

Cloud

Cloud

Cloud

New Freshwater
Sources

The Big Data
Reservoir

Third Eye Blind

The time and engineering effort required to navigate old data sources through the canal will frequently exceed the effort to run a Hadoop job, which itself is no small task. Hadoop is a powerful programming platform, but it is not an application platform. Some customers are surprised to find their Hadoop cluster comes from the factory empty. This is the DIY part of it: even if you buy a dedicated hardware appliance for Hadoop, it doesn't come with the applications that your business requires to analyze your data.

Doing it yourself involves having a competent team of engineers who are capable of both loading the data and writing the applications to process that data. These developers must construct a processing workflow that is responsible for generating the insight. The cast of developers required includes data scientists, workflow engineers (data wranglers), and cluster engineers who keep the supercomputers fed and clothed.

Clusters are loaded two ways: from all the existing stranded sources and with greenfield sources (such as a gaggle of web server logs). Moving old data from the existing stranded sources is often an underfunded project of astonishing complexity. Like any major canal project, the construction of a data canal between legacy sources and the new reservoir will be a complex platform project in its own right.

Migrating large amounts of data is particularly annoying because old systems need to continue to run unimpeded during migration, so accessing those systems is a delicate problem. This third migration platform is hidden from view and must architecturally serve two masters while moving data quickly and carefully. It can be so difficult that even moving a modest amount of data (for example, 30 TB of patient records from an old DB2 mainframe into a Hadoop cluster) will feel like moving passengers off a bus that explodes if it slows down.

Spectrum of Analytic Visibility

Chocolate or vanilla, analog versus digital—it seems as if big data only comes in two flavors, structured and unstructured, but structure lives on a spectrum of analytic visibility into the data. Video data is frequently cited as an unstructured data source, but is seriously structured. An MPEG transport stream contains all sorts of bits to help a set-top box find the correct audio and video streams. Within those streams, there is enough "structure" for a set-top box to disentangle the audio and video streams. The degree of structure required depends on what is to be discovered. A set-top box must be aware of many layers of structure within the bit-stream, whereas an analyst running a big data job to search for criminals in CCTV footage is only interested in the odd macro block and doesn't care if the sound locks to picture.

NoSQL databases have become popular for their affordability and ease of use while operating at internet scale. The organization of data found in the family of noSQL databases is often pejoratively described as unstructured, but a better way to describe it is simply structured. Viewed from deep within a complex and expensive relational database, this simple structure might seem completely unstructured, but the amount of structure required depends entirely on where and what is being looked for and how fast it must be found.

As far back as the 1960s, there was a need to access information in a way that was simple and fast, yet not necessarily sequentially. This method was called the index sequential access method. Access method is a term still used today inside database engines to describe how data is read from tables. An ISAM file had a single index key that could be used to randomly access single records, instead of using a ponderous sequential scan. A user supplied a key and values that were associated with that key were returned to the user. An ISAM-like, key-value table can also be constructed in an enterprise-grade relational database as a simple table, but it is going to be an expensive key-value table, and this is what limits its size, not the inability of the enterprise engine's ability to construct it.

The easiest way to access hundreds of terabytes of data requires access methods to be simple (and by implication, scalable). Simple and scalable requires a relatively simple method like key-value pair. The new generation of fast and cheap noSQL databases now being used for big data applications are also known as key-value pair databases. The structural antithesis of noSQL is the class of complex and expensive uberSQL relational databases.

Big data is about the workflow of cleaning, filtering, and analyzing patterns that lead to discovery. Overly structured data, by definition, has been editorialized, refined, and transformed. With the ability to aggregate so much raw data and all the intermediate steps (including the mistakes) and the final "clean" data, a big data reservoir exposes the workflow. The more this workflow (as ugly as it might be) is exposed to scientists, business owners, and data wranglers, the greater the potential to discover things they didn't know they should have been looking for in the first place. This puts the epiphany into big data.

Historically, the process was called extract, transform, and load (ETL). But the economics and scale of Hadoop have changed the order to ELT since the raw data is loaded before the scheduling power of Map/Reduce can be brought to bear on multiple transform pipelines. Hadoop users have already discovered that the ability to clean up processing pipelines alone justifies the acquisition of a Hadoop cluster. In these cases, analysis must still be conducted in old legacy database silos and re-tooling the analysis pipelines tends to be more difficult. Hadoop also redefines ETL to ELTP, where the P stands for Park. The raw data, processed data, and archived data can now all park together in a single, affordable reservoir.

The Cost of Flexibility

Initial attempts at data discovery started on relational databases when enough data had accumulated to make discovery worthwhile. Most relational databases were not designed to handle acre-feet of data—most were designed to be proficient at online transaction processing (OLTP). Eventually, data warehousing capabilities were grafted onto these database engines, but the grafting was difficult and early versions were unsuccessful. These early attempts at analyzing big data were impeded by kernels that had been optimized for hundreds of tables with hundreds of columns, not a few huge tables with just a few columns and billions of rows.

Eventually, traditional database vendors developed effective methods for handling queries on huge tables, but this resulted in more structure than necessary. A relational data model (or schema) is a collection of tables with various columns. This model provided far more flexibility than the approach it replaced (IBM's IMS hierarchical data model from the 1970s), yet relational technology still required users to know—ahead of time—which columns went into what tables.

Common relational database design encouraged a practice called normalization, which maximized flexibility in case users needed to add new tables or new columns to existing tables. Normalization also minimized the duplication of data between tables because disk space was expensive. This flexibility is why the relational database quickly replaced hierarchical database technology that had been the de facto database up until that point.

SQL queries frequently require many tables to be joined together. The piece of magic inside the database kernel that makes this possible is called the SQL query parser/optimizer or cost-based optimizer (CBO). SQL optimizers use algorithms to determine the cost of retrieving the data in order to select the most cost-effective retrieval strategy. Joining all these tables together to solve the query quickly is a torturous exercise in pretzel logic. A CBO engineered for highly normalized OLTP schemas is designed to join complex tables with thousands of rows. It was not designed for big data schemas that have simpler tables with billions of rows. OLTP-based CBOs optimize space for time, whereas big data CBOs must optimize time for space.

Big data workloads consist of a broad spectrum of purpose-built workloads. This has spawned a myriad of new database products that work at scale but are purpose-built because it is not possible to build a single, general-purpose database kernel or CBO to handle the entire spectrum. In their attempts to address big data with general-purpose warehouse products, customers often end up purchasing "one of each," only to have each attempt result in yet another stranded water tank of data.

By the early 2000s, vast quantities of enterprise data were stranded on software and hardware platforms that were never designed for big data. Even the software and hardware components that were capable of big data (and had re-tooled their CBO to handle billion-row tables) were so expensive that big data would be better described as Big Bucks. Large pools of data that need discovery or that need to be combined with pools from other uberSQL repositories have been trapped in slow, complex, and expensive databases. Building diversion canals between these stranded water towers and the big data reservoir will be difficult, but once fully charged, a reservoir that finally aggregates the data in a single, scalable repository for a single analytic view will be the most important legacy of big data.

CHAPTER 5

Cloudy with a Chance of Meatballs: When Clouds Meet Big Data

The Big Tease

As scientific and commercial supercomputing collide with public and private clouds, the ability to design and operate data centers full of computers is poorly understood by enterprises not used to handling 300 million *anythings*. The promise of a fully elastic and cost-effective computing plant is quite seductive, but Yahoo!, Google, and Facebook solved these problems on their own terms. More conventional enterprises that are now facing either internet-scale computing or a desire to improve the efficiency of their enterprise-scale physical plant will need to identify their own requirements for cloud computing and big data.

Conventional clouds are a form of platform engineering designed to meet very specific and mostly operational requirements. Many clouds are designed by residents of silos that only value the requirements of their own silo. Clouds, like any platform, can be designed to meet a variety of requirements beyond the purely operational. Everyone wants an elastic platform (or cloud), but as discussed in Chapter 2, designing platforms at internet scale always comes with trade-offs, and elasticity does not come free or easy. Big data clouds must meet stringent performance and scalability expectations, which require a very different form of cloud.

The idea of clouds "meeting" big data or big data "living in" clouds isn't just marketing hype. Because big data followed so closely on the trend of cloud computing, both customers and vendors still struggle to understand the differences from their enterprise-centric perspectives. On the surface there are physical similarities in the two technologies—racks of cloud servers and racks of Hadoop servers are constructed from the same physical components. But Hadoop transforms those servers into a single 1000-node supercomputer, whereas conventional clouds host thousands of private mailboxes.

Conventional clouds consist of applications such as mailboxes and Windows desktops and web servers because those applications no longer saturate commodity servers. Cloud technology made it possible to stack enough mailboxes onto a commodity server so that it could achieve operational efficiency. However, Hadoop easily saturates every piece of hardware it can get its hands on, so Hadoop is a bad fit for a conventional cloud that is used to containing many idle applications. Although everyone who already has existing conventional clouds seems to think big data should just work in them effortlessly, it's never that easy. Hadoop clouds must be designed to support supercomputers, not idle mailboxes.

A closer look reveals important differences between conventional clouds and big data; most significantly, they achieve scalability in very different ways, for very different reasons. Beyond the mechanisms of scalability that each exploits, the desire to put big data into clouds so it all operates as one fully elastic supercomputing platform overlooks the added complexity that results from this convergence. Complexity impedes scalability.

Scalability 101

Stated simply, the basic concept of scalability defines how well a platform handles a flood of new customers, more friends, or miles of CCTV footage. Achieving scalability requires a deep understanding about what the platform is attempting to accomplish and how it does that. When a river of new users or data reaches flood stage, a platform scales if it can continue to handle the increased load quickly and cost-effectively.

Although the concept of scalability is easy to understand, the strategies and mechanisms used to achieve scalability for a given set of workloads is complex and controversial, often involving philosophical arguments about how to share things—data, resources, time, money—you know, the usual stuff that humans don't share well. How systems and processes scale isn't merely a propeller-head computer science topic; scalability applies to barbershops, fast food restaurants, and vast swaths of the global economy. Any business that wants to grow understands why platforms need to scale; understanding how to make them scale is the nasty bit.

The most common notion of scalability comes from outside the data center, in economies of scale. Building cars, burgers, or googleplexes requires a means of production that can cost-effectively meet the growth in demand. In the 20th century, the US economy had an affluent population of consumers who comprised a market so large that if a company's product developed a national following, it had to be produced at scale.

This tradition of scalable production traces back past Henry Ford, past the War of Independence, and into the ancestral home of the industrial revolution in Europe. During a minor tiff over a collection of colonies, the British Army felt the need to exercise some moral suasion. Their field rifles were serious pieces of engineering—nearly works of art. They were very high quality, both expensive to build and difficult to maintain in the field. The US army didn't have the engineering or financial resources to build rifles anywhere near that quality, but they knew how to build things simply, cheaply, and with sufficient quality —and these are the tenets of scalable manufacturing.

The only catch to simple, quick, and cheap is quality—not enough quality and the rifles aren't reliable (will it fire after being dropped in a ditch?), and too much quality means higher costs, resulting in fewer weapons. The British had museum-quality rifles, but if that did not translate into more dead Americans, the quality was wasted and therefore not properly optimized. This is the first lesson of doing things at scale: too much quality impedes scale and too little results in a lousy body count.

Scalability isn't just about doing things faster; it's about enabling the growth of a business and being able to juggle the chainsaws of margins, quality, and cost. Pursuit of scalability comes with its own perverse form of disruptive possibilities. Companies that create a great product or service can only build a franchise if things scale, but as their business grows, they often switch to designing for margins instead of market share. This is a great way to drive profit growth until the franchise is threatened.

Choosing margins over markets is a reasonable strategy in tertiary sectors that are mature and not subject to continuous disruption. However, computing technology will remain immature, innovative, and disruptive for some time. It is hard to imagine IT becoming as mature as bridge building, but the Golden Gate bridge was built by the lunatics of their time. Companies that move too far down the margins path can rarely switch back to a market-driven path and eventually collapse under their own organizational weight. The collapse of a company is never fun for those involved, but like the collapse of old stars, the resultant supernova ejects talent out into the market to make possible the next wave of innovative businesses.

Motherboards and Apple Pie

Big data clusters achieve scalability based on pipelining and parallelism, the same assembly line principles found in fast food kitchens. The McDonald brothers applied the assembly line to burgers to both speed up production and reduce the cost of a single burger. Their assembly line consists of several burgers in various states of parallel assembly. In the computer world, this is called pipelining. Pipelining also helps with efficiency by breaking the task of making burgers into a series of simpler steps. Simple steps require less skill; incremental staff could be paid less than British rifle makers (who would, of course, construct a perfect burger). More burgers plus faster plus less cost per burger equals scalability.

In CPU design, breaking down the circuitry pipeline that executes instructions allows that pipeline to run at higher speeds. Whether in a kitchen or a CPU, simple steps make it possible to either reduce the effort required (price) or increase the production (performance) of burgers or instructions. Scalable systems require price and performance to be optimized (not just price and not just performance), all while trying to not let the bacteria seep into the meat left on the counter. Well, that's the theory.

Once a kitchen is setup to efficiently make a series of burgers, then adding another burger assembly line with another grill and more staff to operate it will double the output of the kitchen. It is important to get the first assembly line as efficient as possible when it's the example for thousands of new restaurants. Back inside the CPU, it made economic sense for designers to build multiple floating-point functional units because most of the scientific code that was being run by their customers was saturating the CPU with these instructions. Adding another floating point "grill" made the program run twice as fast and customers gladly paid for it.

Scientific and commercial supercomputing clusters are mostly about parallelism with a little bit of pipelining on the side. These clusters consist of hundreds of "grills" all cooking the data in parallel, and this produces extraordinary scalability. Each cluster node performs exactly the same task (which is more complicated than applying mustard and ketchup), but the cluster contains hundreds of identically configured computers all running exactly the same job on their private slices of data.

Being and Nothingness

Big data cluster software like Hadoop breaks up the analysis of a single, massive dataset into hundreds of identical steps (pipelining) and then runs hundreds of copies at once (parallelism). Unlike what happens in a conventional cloud, Hadoop is not trying to cook hundreds of burgers; it's trying to cook one massive burger. The ability to mince the problem and then charbroil it all together is where the genius lies in commodity supercomputing.

System designers use the term "shared-nothing" to indicate the process of hundreds of nodes working away on the problem while trying not to bother other nodes. Shared-nothing nodes try hard not to share anything. In practice, they do a little sharing, but only enough to propagate the illusion of a single, monolithic supercomputer. On the other hand, shared-everything data architectures emphasize the value gained by having all nodes see a common set of data. Software and hardware mechanisms are required to insure the single view remains correct or coherent but these mechanisms reduce isolation. The need to insure a single, shared view is traded for scalability. There is a class of workloads that does benefit from a single shared view, but in the world of big data, massive scalability is the last thing to be traded away, so shared nothing it is.

When doubled in size, a shared-nothing cluster that scales perfectly operates twice as fast or the job completes in half the time. A shared-nothing cluster never scales perfectly, but getting a cluster to 80% faster when doubled is still considered good scaling. Several platform and workload engineering optimization strategies could be employed to increase the efficiency of a cluster from 80% to 90%. A cluster that scales better remains smaller, which also improves its operational efficiency as well. Hadoop has already been demonstrated to scale to very high node counts (thousands of nodes). But since a 500-node cluster generates more throughput than a 450-node cluster, whether it is 8% faster instead of 11% isn't as important as Hadoop's ability to scale beyond thousands of nodes. Very few data processing platforms can achieve that, let alone do it affordably.

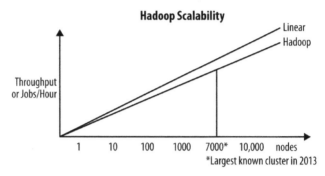

Parity Is for Farmers

Hadoop has done for commercial supercomputing what had already been accomplished in scientific supercomputing in the 1990s. Monolithic HPC supercomputers have been around since the 1960s when Seymour Cray designed the Control Data 6600, which is considered one of the first successful supercomputers. He must have worked as a short-order cook in a previous lifetime since his design innovations resemble those from a fast food kitchen. What made the 6600 fast was the pipelining of tasks within the CPU. The steps were broken down to make them easier and cheaper to design and build. After Cray had finished pipelining the CPU circuits, he turned to parallelism by adding extra burger grills designed specifically to increase the number of mathematical or floating-point results that could be calculated in a second.

After Cray left CDC, he took his design one step further in the Cray-1 by noticing that solving hundreds of equations generated thousands of identical instructions (add two floating numbers, divide by a third). The only difference between all these instructions was the values (or operands) used for each instruction. He decided to build a vector-functional unit that would perform 64 sets of calculations at once—burger's up!

Pipelining and parallelism have been hallmarks of HPC systems like the Cray, but very few corporations could afford a Cray or an IBM mainframe. Decades later, microprocessors became both affordable and capable enough that if you could figure out how to lash a hundred of them together, you might have a shot at creating a poor man's Cray. In the late 1980s, software technology was developed to break up large monolithic jobs designed to run on a Cray into a hundred smaller jobs. It wasn't long before some scheduling software skulking around a university campus in the dead of night was infesting a network of idle workstations. If a single workstation was about 1/50th the speed of a Cray, then you only needed 50 workstations to break even. Two hundred workstations were four times faster than the Cray and the price/performance was seriously good, especially since another department probably paid for those workstations.

Starting with early Beowulf clusters in the 1990s, HPC clusters were being constructed from piles of identically configured commodity servers (i.e., pipeline simplicity). Today in 2013, a 1000-node HPC cluster constructed from nodes that have 64 CPU cores and zillions of memory controllers can take on problems that could only be dreamed about in the 1990s.

Google in Reverse

Hadoop software applies the HPC cluster trick to a class of internet-scale computing problems that are considered non-scientific. Hadoop is an evolution of HPC clusters for a class of non-scientific workloads that were plaguing companies with internet-scale, non-scientific datasets. Financial services and healthcare companies also had problems as large as the HPC crowd, but until Hadoop came along, the only way to analyze their big data was with relational databases.

Hadoop evolved directly from commodity scientific supercomputing clusters developed in the 1990s. Hadoop consists of a parallel execution framework called Map/Reduce and Hadoop Distributed File System (HDFS). The file system and scheduling capabilities in Hadoop were primarily designed to operate on, and be tolerant of, unreliable commodity components. A Hadoop cluster could be built on eight laptops pulled from a dumpster and it would work—not exactly at enterprise grade, but it would work. Yahoo! couldn't initially afford to build 1000-node clusters with anything other than the cheapest subcomponents, which is the first rule of assembly lines anyway; always optimize the cost and effort of the steps in the pipeline. Hadoop was designed to operate on terabytes of data spread over thousands of flaky nodes with thousands of flaky drives.

Hadoop makes it possible to build large commercial supercomputing platforms that scale to thousands of nodes and, for the first time, scale affordably. A Hadoop cluster is a couple of orders of magnitude (hundreds of times) cheaper than platforms built on relational technology and, in most cases, the price/performance is several orders of magnitude (thousands of times) better. What happened to the big-iron, expensive HPC business in the early 1990s will now happen to the existing analytics and data warehouse business. The scale and price/performance of Hadoop is significantly disrupting both the economics and nature of how business analytics is conducted.

Isolated Thunderstorms

Everybody understands the value gained from a high-resolution view of consumers' shopping habits or the possibility of predicting where crimes are likely to take place. This value is realized by analyzing massive piles of data. Hadoop must find a needle, customer, or criminal in a large haystack and do it quickly. Hadoop breaks up one huge haystack into hundreds of small piles of hay. The act of isolating the haystacks into smaller piles creates a scalable, shared-nothing environment so that all the hundreds of piles are searched simultaneously.

Superficially, Hadoop seems to be related to cloud computing because the first cloud implementations came from the same companies attempting internet-scale computing. The isolation benefits that make any shared-nothing platform achieve scalability also make clouds scale. However, clouds and Hadoop achieve isolation through very different mechanisms. The Hadoop isolation mechanism breaks up a single pile of hay into hundreds of piles so each one of those nodes works on its own private pile. Hadoop creates synthesized isolation. But a cloud running a mail application that supports hundreds of millions of users already started out with hundreds of millions of mailboxes or little piles of hay. Conventional clouds have natural isolation. The isolation mechanism results from the initial requirement that each email user is isolated from the others for privacy. Although Hadoop infrastructure looks very similar to the servers running all those mailboxes, Hadoop clusters remain one single, monolithic supercomputer disguised as a collection of cheap, commodity servers.

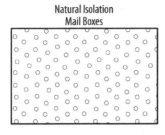

Natural Isolation
Mail Boxes

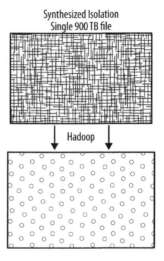

Synthesized Isolation
Single 900 TB file

Hadoop

The Myth of Private Clouds

Cloud computing evolved from grid computing, which evolved from client-server computing, and so on, back to the IBM Selectric. Operating private clouds remains undiscovered country for most enterprises. Grids at this scale are not simply plumbing; they are serious adventures in modern engineering. Enterprises mostly use clouds to consolidate their sprawling IT infrastructure and to reduce costs. Many large enterprises in the 1990s had hundreds or thousands of PCs that needed care and feeding, which mostly meant installing, patching, and making backups. As the workforce became more mobile and laptops replaced desktops, employees' computers and employers' sensitive data became more difficult to protect. Early private clouds were set up to move everyone's "My Documents" folder back into their data center so it could be better secured, backed up, and restored.

When personal computers began to have more computing power than the servers running the back-office accounting systems, most of the spare power went unused by those users who spent their days using MS Office. A single modern workstation in the early 2000s could support 8 or 10 users. This "bare iron" workstation could be carved up into 10 virtual PCs using a hypervisor like VMware's ESX or Red Hat's KVM. Each user got about the same experience as having their own laptop gave them, but the company reduced costs.

Conventional clouds consist of thousands of virtual servers, and as long as nothing else is on your server beating the daylights out of it, you're good to go. The problem with running Hadoop on clouds of virtualized servers is that it beats the crap out of bare-iron servers for a living. Hadoop achieves impressive scalability with shared-nothing isolation techniques, so Hadoop clusters hate to share hardware with anything else. Share no data and share no hardware—Hadoop is shared-nothing.

While saving money is a worthwhile pursuit, conventional cloud architecture is still a complicated exercise in scalable platform engineering. Many private conventional clouds will not be able to support Hadoop because they rely on each individual application to provide its own isolation. Hadoop in a cloud means large, pseudo-monolithic supercomputer clusters lumbering around. Hadoop is not elastic like millions of mailboxes can be. It is a 1000-node supercomputer cluster that thinks (or maybe wishes) it is still a Cray. Conventional clouds designed for mailboxes can be elastic but will not elastically accommodate supercomputing clusters that, as a single unit of service, span 25 racks.

It's not that Hadoop can't run on conventional clouds—it can and will run on a cloud built from dumpster laptops, but your SLA mileage will vary a lot. Performance and scalability will be severely compromised by underpowered nodes connected to underpowered external arrays or any other users running guests on the physical servers that contain Hadoop data nodes. A single Hadoop node can easily consume physical servers, even those endowed with 1300+ MB/sec of disk I/O throughput.

A Tiny Data 8-node bare-iron cluster can produce over 10GB/sec. Most clouds share I/O and network resources based on assumptions that guests will never be as demanding as Hadoop data nodes are. Running Hadoop in a conventional cloud will melt down the array because of the way that most SANs are configured and connected to clouds in enterprises. Existing clouds that were designed, built, and optimized for web servers, email, app servers, and Windows desktops simply will not be able to support Hadoop clusters.

The network fabric of a Hadoop cluster is the veins and arteries of HDFS and must be designed for scalable throughput—not attachment and manageability, which is the default topology for conventional clouds and most enterprise networks. If Hadoop is imposed on a conventional cloud, it needs to be a cloud designed to run virtual supercomputers in the first place, not a conventional cloud that has been remodeled, repurposed, and reshaped. Big data clouds have to be designed for big data.

My Other Data Center Is an RV Park

Companies attempting to build clouds or big data platforms that operate at internet-scale are discovering they need to rethink everything they thought they knew about how to design, build, and run data centers. The internet-scale pioneering companies initially purchased servers from vendors like IBM, HP, and Dell, but quickly realized that the value, and therefore pricing, of those servers was driven by features they didn't need (like graphics chips and RAID cards).

The same features that might be useful for regular customers became completely irrelevant to companies that were going to sling 85,000 servers without ever running a stitch of Windows. Hardware vendors were building general-purpose servers so that their products would appeal to the greatest number of customers. This is a reasonable convention in product design, but like scientific computing users, commercial computing users do not require general-purpose servers to construct purpose-built supercomputing platforms.

At internet-scale, absolutely everything must be optimized, including everything in the computing plant. After learning how to buy or build stripped-down servers, these companies quickly moved on to optimizing the entire notion of a data center, which is just as critical as the server and software to the platform. It was inevitable that the physical plant also had to be deconstructed and optimized.

Today's data centers can be found in a stack of intermodal containers like those on an ocean freighter. Because a container full of computers only needs power, water for cooling, and a network drop, data centers can also be located on empty lots or abandoned RV parks.

Converge Conventionally

Cloud computing evolved from the need to handle millions of free email users cheaply. Big data evolved from a need to solve an emerging set of supercomputing problems. Grids or clouds or whatever they will be called in the future are simply platforms of high efficiency and scale.

Although clouds are primarily about the operational aspects of a computing plant, learning how to operate a supercomputer is not like operating any traditional IT platform. Managing platforms at this scale is extremely disruptive to the enterprise's notion of what it means to operate computers. And over time, the care and feeding of thousands of supercomputers will eventually lead us to change the way computers must operate.

CHAPTER 6

Haystacks and Headgames

The Demise of Counting

So far, I have been discussing how big data differs from previous methods of computing—how it provides benefits and creates disruptions. Even at this early stage, it is safe to predict that big data will become a multibillion-dollar analytics and BI business and possibly subsume the entire existing commercial ecosystem. During that process, it will have disrupted the economics, behavior, and understanding of everything it analyzes and everyone who touches it—from those who use it to model the biochemistry of personality disorders to agencies that know the color of your underwear.

Big data is going to lay enough groundwork that it will initiate another set of much larger changes to the economics and science of computing. (But the future will always contain elements from the past, so mainframes, tape, and disks will still be with us for a while.) This chapter is going to take a trip into the future and imagine what the post-big data world might look like. The future will require us to process zettabytes and yottabytes of data on million-node clusters. In this world, individual haystacks will be thousands of times the size of the largest Hadoop clusters that will be built in the next decade. We are going to discover what the end of computing might look like, or more precisely, the end of counting.

The first electronic computers were calculators on steroids, but still just calculators. When you had something to calculate, you programmed the machinery, fed it some data, and it did the counting. Early computers that solved mathematical equations for missile trajectory still had to solve these equations using simple math. Solving an equation the way a theoretical physicist might is how human brains solve equations, but computers don't work like brains. There have been attempts at building computers that mimic the way brains solve equations, but engineering constraints make it more practical to build a hyperactive calculator that solves equations through brute force and ignorance.

Modern processors now operate with such brute force (i.e., clock speed) and the ignorance of simple electronics that can add, subtract, multiply, and divide with every clock tick. On a good day, this could be 12 billion every second. If processors that have 16 cores could be fed data fast enough (hint: they can't), this would be 192 billion calculations/second. The software that made the algebraic method possible still runs on those crazy counting machines. Lucky for us, we can still get a lot accomplished with brute force and ignorance.

Scientific computing clusters have to solve problems so immense that they are constructed from thousands of multi-core processors. The NOAA weather forecasting supercomputer is a good example, but despite the immense computing power, weather forecasters still long for a supercomputer that is hundreds of thousands of times more powerful. Hadoop supercomputers follow in the architectural footsteps of these powerhouse-modeling machines, but instead of predicting hurricanes, commercial supercomputers are searching through haystacks of data for patterns. They're looking to see if you bought Prada shoes after your Facebook friend bought a pair. In order for Facebook to deliver more targeted consumers to advertisers, their Hadoop supercomputers break up your own data and your friends' information haystacks into thousands of piles and analyze every single piece of straw looking for connections and patterns among shopping habits and social behavior.

Early experiences of data pattern analysis began to reveal connections and started to answer questions that were not previously being asked. From electoral campaigns to insurance providers and restaurant chains, everyone has discovered new questions to ask big data. For computing platforms built on brute force and ignorance, they were suddenly becoming a lot less ignorant. Traditional supercomputers are still calculators, whereas Hadoop supercomputers are pattern explorers. Computers aren't supposed to be able to predict social behavior.

Another aspect of computing in the 21st century is the rapid and relentless accumulation of data, and big data is just the leading wave of this tsunami. As network connection speeds to consumers increase further, data transforms from basic text and logs to graphics and eventually HD video in 3D. With 40 to 70 percent of the human brain dedicated to visual processing, the web will continue to become a high-resolution visual experience, further disrupting what it means to broadcast and entertain, because that is the fastest way to transmit information to a human (for example, it's faster to tell time from an analog watch than it is to read digits).

Text consumes little space—this small book would fit onto an old floppy disk if I could find one—but visual information requires millions of megabytes. Processing visual data and eventually "teaching" computers to "see" images starts to hint at the computational problems ahead. In a few short years, Hadoop has gone from looking at strings of characters to macro-blocks of video as it transitioned from being a tool for discovery to a tool for seeing and understanding what it is processing.

Lose the Haystack

Big data tools will continue to be useful for a few more years before they usher in the era of Super-Sized Data. Advances in conventional computing technology will extend the life of many clusters. Processors within early clusters were expensive, consumed a lot of power, and were designed to run software from another era. In commercial supercomputing, analysis is limited by how fast the data can be pulled into a processor, quickly scanned for patterns, and then discarded to make room for the next chunk. Processors designed for that other era became overheated and underemployed memory controllers.

The generation of extremely low-power, cheap processors that are optimized around discovering (not calculating) exabytes of data will make it possible to build 100,000-node clusters. A cluster this size will again push the frontiers of what can be discovered, but in the world where exabytes of high-resolution visual data needs to be "seen," the superior scalability first made famous by scientific clusters and then by Hadoop will not be enough. We need to stop looking for the needle in the haystack by looking at every piece of straw—we need to stop counting.

The current approach to computing is based on ideas from John Von Neumann, who is generally credited for the way computers work today. In a Hadoop cluster, every piece of data is still inspected, and if the pieces remain small, 100,000-node ARM clusters will be able to extend the shelf life of current "inspecting" clusters. If each piece of hay is a tweet or a zip code, then the pieces are small. If each piece of hay is three hours of full-motion HD video, the computing problem of inspecting starts to move out of reach even for these massive clusters. When the cluster has to "see" all the data instead of just inspecting it, then we need to create more scalable strategies.

Mind Another Gap

The human brain has long been recognized as a unique form of supercomputer. In a crude sense, it is a 50 billion-node cluster that consists of very high-resolution analog logic combined with a digital FM transmission fabric between all the nodes. A neuron fires when enough chemical signals have accumulated across all of its synaptic gaps. The neuron can be held in a state where it is waiting for the last molecule to arrive before it will fire. When the last molecule of neurotransmitter is dumped into one of the many synaptic gaps, the neuron finally fires.

Your 50-billion-node supercomputer has neurons that have a trigger resolution that is sensitive to a single molecule, and there are hundreds of trillions of molecules in your brain. Some of the neurochemicals come from the things you ingest and some from the RNA of the cells that are responsible for creating the amino acids that become neurotransmitters. Trying to solve problems like why people get Alzheimer's are not yet within reach. Alzheimer's is an autoimmune disease where the person's own brain chemistry attacks the wiring between the neurons. This disease destroys the fabric and so destroys the person. Researchers believe that each neural cell is a sophisticated chemical computer in its own right. Many brain chemicals come from RNA expression and some come from your café latte. All of the genetic and environmental chemical processes band together to make up your charming self.

Combined with the sheer number of neurons and their interconnection, the problem of modeling a human brain with enough accuracy to answer questions about why people develop schizophrenia, fall in love, or feel more productive after drinking coffee requires all of the brain's biochemistry to be simulated. However, the computing technology needs to advance far beyond even the largest conventional supercomputers we could ever construct. Like weather forecasters, neurologists can never have enough computing power.

The exponential growth in the amount of data and the scope of problems that need attention must be met with an exponential advancement in the science of counting things. In the future, there will be many problems that a modest 100 million-node Hadoop cluster can tackle, but modeling the human cortex won't be one of them—we have to stop counting things. So, what might the next step be for computing? It will still involve some of the parlor tricks already found in Hadoop clusters, but will also need to steal a few from the supercomputer you are using now—your noodle.

Believing Is Seeing

My personal interest in neuroscience started because I was born with Sturge-Weber Syndrome, a rare developmental disorder. Nobody knows what causes SWS yet, so it's a good candidate to simulate when we get our brain cluster built. Its most common symptom is a port-wine stain on the face. The birthmark is caused by an overabundance of capillaries just under the surface of the skin. The instructions for creating the right number of capillaries somehow gets messed up during development. If the foul-up occurs along the outer branches of the fifth cranial nerve, the result is a port-wine stain.

If the mistake occurs further up the line and closer to the cortex, then the brain itself ends up with a port-wine stain of sorts, and this is when the syndrome becomes lethal. Some newborns with the cortical version of SWS have seizures right after birth and must have sections of their cortex removed with a hemispherectomy in order to stop the seizures. It is a testament to both the extraordinary elasticity of the cortex and the relentless, built-in will to survive that some patients can survive this operation, recover, and thrive.

My SWS affected the retina of my right eye. The human eye has a complex internal network of capillaries that nourish the photoreceptors. These vessels sit in front of the retina (which is why you see flashes of blood vessels when a doctor shines in a light). My port-wine stain wasn't in my cortex, but it was on my face and in my retina. My right eye wasn't very healthy and I eventually lost sight in it when I was 12. Adolescence is a tough time for many people, but I had to relearn how to see and do simple things like hit a baseball or walk down a crowded hallway. I would later understand the neuroscience and cognitive processes that were taking place, but it turned out that I spent my wasted youth rewiring my cortex.

Simple things like walking down that hallway became my supercomputing problem to solve. As a kid, I was a good baseball player, but fell into a hitting slump after I became monocular. As I slowly relearned how to hit, at some point it became easier because I stopped "seeing" with my eye and started seeing with my muscles and body position. Coaches call it spatial intelligence and encourage players to develop that skill for many sports, including hitting and pitching. My brain had to become more spatially intelligent just to walk down the hallway. In order to locate a pitch in the strike zone (within an inch or so), precise and repeated location of the human body in space is required. In order to have that kind of precision, pitchers are usually born with a natural spatial intelligence. I have a crude version of this intelligence, but nowhere near the spatial genius that is Mariano Rivera.

The other change my brain had to make was a greater reliance on the right hemisphere that is responsible for spatial processing. This hemisphere must do a lot more spatial work when it is fed with only one eye's worth of data. The brain is a stereo device, so with one eye, half the data went missing and then another chunk was lost going from stereo to mono vision. In order to see, I have to imagine or model a 3D world. Over time, my brain learned to synthesize a three-dimensional world from a limited amount of two-dimensional data. I was born left-handed and when I became left-eyed at 12, I became right-brained for both seeing and thinking.

A good example of how well my (and other brains) can spatially model the world occurs when I have to drive at night in the rain. I should not be able to do this, and must fully exploit every spatial trick to pull it off. I battle with low light (no data), deep shadows (contrast flare), and reflections (visual noise) from wet road surfaces. All these obstacles result in very little roadway telemetry coming through the windshield. I can't possibly see everything that goes by, so I imagine what safely driving down the freeway might look like and then look for aberrations in the visual field and use this visual information to correct my internal model. I had to become a spatial supercomputer to survive, but humans with stereovision are also spatial supercomputers—I just need a few extra plugins. For me, the cliché "I'll believe it when I see it" has become "I'll see it when I believe it."

Unlike supercomputers, human brains never examine every piece of hay but have well-developed strategies like associative memory, habituated learning, and a retina (even a single one) that can reduce data by orders of magnitude. Brains only look at things that might be interesting. The future of computing is also going to have to stop sifting through haystacks, and that means saying goodbye to Dr. von Neumann.

Spatial Intelligence

One of the drawbacks of studying the brain from a computer-centric perspective is that pretending the brain works like a computer is deceptively convenient. Although neuroscience has made recent and excellent progress, it is still a fairly young science. To be fair to neurologists, they have to decipher a 50 billion-node supercomputer using their own 50 billion-node supercomputers, where no two clusters have exactly the same version of the operating system and there is no shortage of bugs. The next generation of electronic supercomputers will need to adapt some strategies from the central nervous system that were perfected after doing live QA for millions of years.

The CNS is easily distracted and lazy—probably not a fan of big data since it is ruthless about ignoring data that is no longer interesting. It is interrupt-driven and gets quickly bored with static data. An experiment you can do with one closed eye is to put gentle pressure on the side of the open eyeball. This temporarily stops the involuntary jitter motion of the eye positioning muscles and causes the visual field to slowly fade to black. The eye muscles constantly need to get the attention of the photoreceptors or your world fades away. The neural technique of ignoring data is called habituation. Data that is not changing is no longer novel. Because the CNS is designed to be easily distracted, when the balance between habituation and novelty becomes disrupted, disorders like ADD can result.

The eye has about 110 million photoreceptors, but there are only about one million cables running to the visual cortex, so the reduction in data between what the jittery retinas receive and what they push upstream is immense. Retinas together spatially encode information like the width of a hallway that must be navigated. Seeing with two retinas makes this encoding extremely precise, whereas the precision in my case must be calculated in the cortex. If I'm tired, sick, or tipsy, then I start to make seeing mistakes. By performing this processing in two healthy retinas, the visual cortex is free to concentrate on looking for someone familiar in a crowded hallway. The human brain can recognize familiar faces at speeds exceeding the threshold of human perception. The CNS processes and encodes information at the source, without the need to bring all of the data into the brain. There is a lot of computing happening in the periphery, and this is what differentiates brain architecture from the conventional and centralized counting architectures of computers.

The human brain is a ridiculously powerful spatial supercomputer, driven by a crafty, lazy, and easily distracted nervous system. Recent FMRI studies of humans playing or even just listening to music reveals large swaths of the brain lighted like a Christmas tree—we don't know why music is so important to humans, but we do know that the brain on music is one very happy supercomputer. Put high-performance athletes into an FMRI and watch more happy computers at work. Both big data and eventually this emerging form of spatial supercomputing will simultaneously be George Orwell's worst nightmare and Oliver Sacks' dream come true.

Associative Supercomputing

The ability to recognize your mother's face in a crowd, in the blink of an eye, depends heavily on how your mother's face was remembered. Associative memory in the brain is critical to the speed of the facial recognition engine. I can't drive down the freeway in the rain at night if I can't imagine what a safe version of what that might look like. I have to have something to compare the crude and incomplete image coming from my retina. That pattern is stored as complex spatial memory consisting of road signs and landmarks. This imagination strategy will not be successful if I can't remember the stretch of road.

The brain is also good at retrieving more than just the stretch of road. Spatial memories also come with other pieces of potentially useful information. A stretch of road might be associated with memories of short on ramps, which have a habit of producing unexpected data in the form of accelerating vehicles. Unexpected situations need to be minimized, because quickly learning a new situation under impaired operating conditions produces errors in perception and the disruptive possibility of a fender bender.

Associative memory indexing is very easy for a brain, but very difficult using current computing technology. Spatial supercomputers will be much more difficult to build and early versions will still rely heavily on the massive, classic supercomputers. New approaches to both hardware and software design will be required to implement an associative computer that can recognize faces in milliseconds, but I suspect our first 50-billion node cluster probably won't be as small as a cantaloupe either.

Back from the Future

A Hadoop cluster doesn't have to be just about crunching big data. Like HPC clusters, Hadoop works because it busts up a problem into a thousand pieces and works on them in parallel. With big datasets, this is pretty much the only way to fly, but for small datasets, things like Hadoop are equally effective because it is about getting work done in parallel in much less time. Our retinas are like tiny Hadoop clusters. If a Hadoop cluster is put on a tiny board with hundreds of processors and a few TB of memory, then it could be installed into a pair of sunglasses. Brute force and linear parallelism will remain a useful strategy, but figuring out that only five haystacks out of 5000 are worth searching will get us to the next threshold of computing.

As hard as I have tried to dispense with the advances in counting in the last 60 years, the old form of computing won't go away quickly or quietly; nor should it. The new form of computing will not be about counting—it will be a hybrid of classic techniques combined with more crafty ways of processing information that are similar to the ways our brains work. Big data is not always going to be about data, nor is it always going to be about discovery or insight derived from having improved workflows. It is about the intuition that results from the brain visually integrating information so quickly that the workflow becomes unconscious. Whatever the future of computing will be, it almost certainly starts with a name change.

Acknowledgments

I appreciate the authoritative feedback and constructive criticism from my friends and colleagues who have been around since I began writing this book a million years ago: Ed Gasiorowski, Bruce Nelson, Doug Rady, and Rikin Shah.

I cannot express enough gratitude to Douglas Paris White who translated so many of my non-linear thoughts and opinions into a coherent form without diminishing my voice.

Thanks to Cynthia and Georgia for suffering through the writing process with me.

Finally, this book is dedicated to the memory of my friend and mentor, David L. Willingham (1938-2012).

About the Author

Jeffrey Needham is the founder of Scale Abilities, Inc., a Silicon Valley consulting firm, and is an authority in ecosystem engineering at Hortonworks in Palo Alto, California. Informed by three decades of experience in both hardware and software engineering, he is a frequent writer and speaker on topics of database performance and scalability, platform engineering, and advanced cluster design for Hadoop. Customers appreciate Jeff's creative strategies for evaluating and implementing their big data initiatives. He lives with his family in the Santa Cruz mountains.

CPSIA information can be obtained at www.ICGtesting.com
Printed in the USA
LVOW01s2311220913

353567LV00016B/37/P